STRONG
and KIND

STRONG and KIND

And Other Important Character Traits
Your Child Needs to Succeed

KORIE ROBERTSON
with CHRYS HOWARD

THOMAS NELSON
Since 1798

Published in Nashville, Tennessee, by W Publishing Group, an imprint of Thomas Nelson.

Thomas Nelson titles may be purchased in bulk for educational, business, fund-raising, or sales promotional use. For information, please e-mail SpecialMarkets@ ThomasNelson.com.

Unless otherwise noted, Scripture quotations are taken from the Holy Bible, New International Version®, NIV®. © 1973, 1978, 1984, 2011 by Biblica, Inc.® Used by permission of Zondervan. All rights reserved worldwide.

Scripture quotations marked NKJV are taken from the New King James Version®. © 1982 by Thomas Nelson. Used by permission. All rights reserved.

Scripture quotation marked GW is taken from *God's Word*®. © 1995 God's Word to the Nations. Used by permission of Baker Publishing Group. All rights reserved.

Scripture quotations marked NLT are taken from the *Holy Bible*, New Living Translation. © 1996, 2004, 2007, 2013 by Tyndale House Foundation. Used by permission of Tyndale House Publishers, Inc., Carol Stream, Illinois 60189. All rights reserved.

Scripture quotations marked KJV are taken from the King James Version of the Bible.

Italics added to Scripture quotations are the author's own emphasis.

Library of Congress Control Number: 2015943084

ISBN 978-0-7180-3688-1

Printed in the United States of America

15 16 17 18 19 RRD 6 5 4 3 2 1

For our children:
I pray that you will walk through this life with strength and kindness;
that you will always know the love your dad and I have for you is
without condition, without question, overflowing, and never ending;
and that you will realize God loves you even more.
It seems impossible, but it's true.

CONTENTS

PART THREE: HOW TO PARENT KIDS OF CHARACTER

PICK TWO

"What are two important character traits that you want to see in your children?"

I was sitting with a circle of women in a Bible study when this question was posed. I was a mom of two young toddlers, working part-time as the children's minister at our church, happily going to every study group I could find. Sometimes there was a sweet teenager there to watch the kids; if not it was a good excuse to leave the kids to bond with their daddy for an hour or two while I enjoyed some much-needed adult conversation uninterrupted by a child saying "mama" every 2.3 seconds.

Willie and I were young—twenty-three and twenty-one years old, respectively—when we had our firstborn. I had just graduated from college, and Willie still had a few semesters to go. He had started college a semester after I did, having first gone to seminary and then working during our college years while I sped through, eager to start our family.

When John Luke came along in October 1995, we couldn't have been more excited. What a gift! Willie and I, along with our families, absolutely adore babies. John Luke, the first grandchild on my side of the family, was passed up and down the church aisle every Sunday morning. Having been the oldest grandchild, I had lots of experience with little ones. I grew up babysitting my cousins, so I could certainly change diapers and rock a baby to sleep. Plus, I'm a reader, so I not only had experience, but I had read lots of books. I was fully prepared to be a mom. Here's the lovely thing about youth: you don't know what you don't know.

Being a young parent has its advantages. For one thing, you don't know what to worry about. You just do what you have to do. Willie and I had planned and dreamed about the sweet children God would give us; we had talked about how we were raised and how we planned to raise our babies. My family and Willie's family couldn't have looked more different on the outside. (He lived on the river; I lived in a subdivision. He went to public school; I went to private school. He never played little league or took a lesson of any kind. I took lessons in everything, from piano to diving to baton twirling. His dad never came to one of his basketball games in junior high or high school; my parents were always on the sidelines, the VHS video recorder fully charged and ready to capture the moment. His mom is known for her cooking; my mom has the local pizza place on speed dial.) While the methods they used in raising us were certainly far from the same, the values and character traits they instilled in us were from our mutual faith in God. So in that respect our upbringings were the same.

Even with that type of common ground, there are a lot of variations in how parents can raise their babies. Willie and I had a lot to figure out. We weren't really thinking of that at the time, though. We were young and in love and just excited to be having a baby.

The Most Important Thing
for Parents to Decide

After being a parent for twenty years, I have come to believe that the most important thing for parents to decide—more important than bottle- or breastfeeding, more important than co-sleeping or sleep training, and even more important than whether to put your child in day care or become a stay-at-home parent—is what values are important to your family and how you will go about instilling those values in your children.

My dad started a tradition that we continued on every family vacation during my growing-up years. We would go through what he called our "Howard Family Legacy of Principles for Living." (I know, long title. My dad isn't known for his brevity.) I'll admit, in the middle of riding the waves at the beach, hanging out with cousins, or making runs to the arcade at the neighboring hotel, we weren't always that excited about sitting down and going through a list of principles. But my dad always insisted, and for that I am now grateful.

Our Howard Family Legacy of Principles for Living was a list of values that our family held dear and would strive to live by. At some point during every vacation, we would talk through each value we had previously listed and add to the list anything we had learned over the last year and deemed important enough to include. These values were based on the Bible and truths that we, as a family, wanted to keep in the forefront of our minds.

Through the years this list provided a compass for us whenever we forgot who we were and whose we were. It provided that little voice in our heads that reminded us of the kind of people we wanted to be. Check out this list in the appendix and consider starting one for your family. If you do, make it your own. Call it whatever you want. Feel free to take one or two principles as a starting point, and then ask your kids what values they believe are important for your family. This was a great way for our family to pass down a legacy of positive, healthy values, and it can be for yours too.

What Values Do You Hold Dear?

So back to the question posed to me in the women's Bible study. As you can see, the concept of considering values or character traits that are important and living by them wasn't new to me. But that night was the first time I remember actually trying to pinpoint the values I wanted for *our* children. What values did Willie and I hold dear? Not just what we had been taught from our families, but what was important for us, for our own little ones? As I said before, we were young and had, in a few short years, gone from learning these things from our parents to teaching, instilling, and living them in front of our kids.

Our parents had not just *talked* about values that are important, but they also *lived* them, which I believe makes all the difference. My parents followed the principles we discussed on our family vacations. For Willie and me, life was good and peaceful; we knew that both our sets of parents were going to stick together through thick and thin, in sickness and health, and for richer or poorer. We had confidence that God was with us and that His Word was true and a good guide for living full and happy lives. We also knew that although our parents were not perfect, they would always strive to live God's way. Those were the things I wanted for my children then, and although much has changed in our lives since I was a young mom sitting in that Bible study, those are the same things I still want for my children now.

I remember clearly my answer from that night. I hadn't put it into words before then, but I knew immediately that my answer was, "Strong and kind." These were the first two words that came to my mind then, and they are still my answer today. These are the two traits I thought our kids would need to survive in this tough, beautiful world—to maneuver through difficult times and to be the light God has called them to be. If our children grew up to be strong and kind adults, I figured we would have been successful in our role as parents.

But why strong and kind?

THE VALUE OF BEING STRONG

Being strong is essential to me because we know that life in this world is not always easy. Our kids will have people they thought were friends turn on them; they will have loved ones move away or die; they will have times when they won't make the cheerleading squad or their first love will break their heart. As they get older, their marriages will go through tough times; the person they most love will let them down. They may have to deal with miscarriages, job losses, and cancer. Our children are not immune to the problems that make our time in this fallen world so difficult. They need to be strong to get through these times.

Since we know our children will experience these kinds of difficulties, we want to prepare them—to help them become strong enough to handle whatever comes their way. Our strength doesn't come from us but from the One living in us. The Bible tells us to be strong in Him and in His power (Eph. 6:10). We want our children to have the confidence that comes from knowing that when God is for them, no one can be against them (Rom. 8:31). We want them to know that even though tough times will come, there will be good on the other side. They need to know that with God they'll be strong enough to ride out the storm. We want our children to be resilient so if these storms of life bend them, they will not break, and they will always come back to their faith in their Father in heaven.

We want our children to be strong so they won't be swayed by others' opinions of them or easily influenced by peer pressure, social media, or entertainment. We want them to be secure in what they know about themselves and confident that God's way is the best way no matter what the outside influences are saying. We want them to be able to hold firmly to God's values and truth, even in the midst of the voices telling them differently.

The Bible is full of words that encourage us to be strong. One of my favorites is "Have I not commanded you? Be strong and courageous. Do not be afraid; do not be discouraged, for the LORD your God will be with you wherever you go" (Joshua 1:9).

Strong. It was the first trait that came to my mind that day.

THE VALUE OF BEING KIND

My other word was *kind*. This trait is for the benefit of others. Kindness is in direct opposition to concern for one's self. Being kind is all about being thoughtful, noticing another's need and filling it. To be kind is to be loving and gentle with others even when they don't deserve it. It's showing compassion to the hurting and encouraging others' successes. It's using good manners and showing respect for others' thoughts and opinions that differ from yours; it's living a life that is peaceful and joyful.

God is love (1 John 4:8), and the Bible tells us that love is patient *and* kind (1 Cor. 13:4). Our desire is for our children to treat others with kindness, no matter their race, social standing, popularity in school, or religious background. We never know what hard times a person has had or is going through and how valuable a kind word would be to that person.

Since God is love, and love is kind, we want our children to be kind. We want them to make this world a better place, to always leave a place or a person better than they found it. The Bible tells us that caring for widows and orphans is an act of true religion (see James 1:27). We're told that when we feed the hungry or clothe the needy, we're feeding and clothing Jesus Himself (Matt. 25:40). Can you imagine how much better the world would be if people decided to be kinder to one another, to give others the benefit of the doubt, to respond when they see a need, and to offer a kind word rather than responding in the short, rude manner we use too often when we talk with one another when things aren't going our way? Willie and I want our children to have servants' hearts, to love others as they love themselves, and to believe that love and kindness can change the world. That's why I chose kindness as the second trait for our children.

After voicing my desire to instill these two traits in our children, I took my requests to God. I started praying that Willie and I would be able to teach our children these things—that we would raise strong, kind kids who would become strong, kind adults. God spoke to me very clearly. He said, "Then live it." So I started praying that Willie and I would *be* the traits we wanted for our children—that we would live them and model them so that our kids wouldn't just hear empty words from us but would see the fruit of these character traits in our lives.

On What Character Traits Do You Want to Focus?

This is not a book to tell you how to parent your children. Willie and I certainly are not perfect parents, nor do I believe there is a perfect way to parent your child. Families come in all different shapes and sizes, as evidenced by Willie's family and mine. God made each of us to be unique. Aren't we thankful for that? I am one who appreciates differences. I love people with strong opinions, quirky habits, and interesting ways of living. God imprinted in our DNA and impressed on our hearts things that make each of us special. No one else in the world is quite like you as a parent or quite like your children. That's what makes the world go 'round.

This is a book to help you answer this question: What two character traits do you want to focus on and instill in your children? Think about what's important to you. What has God placed on your heart? What principles guide you? What have your own life experiences taught you that your children will need to make it through theirs?

I pray that you will have the confidence to be the unique mom or dad God created you to be to parent your one-of-a-kind child and that there is a little bit of truth somewhere in this book that helps you on your journey.

Willie's Words on Our Two Traits

When I think about being strong and kind, I realize that, like Korie, I grew up seeing and being taught those traits by my own parents. However, I saw them in a different way than she saw them. When you grow up with three brothers in a two-bedroom house on the river, and little money, the characteristic of being strong develops pretty naturally. In fact, it's a necessity. I also saw strong role models in my parents and grandparents, who all had strong personalities and knew the value of hard work. We were taught that no one owes you anything, you're not entitled, and there would be no sympathy for you if you were weak. Yes, four boys in the house meant there was plenty of knocking around going on, so you had better toughen up and get strong.

Growing up, my dad was the epitome of strength. Not only

was he physically strong, having played Division I football in college and running hundreds of hoop nets to catch fish for a living, but he was, and still is, very strong in his beliefs and passions. He wasn't the only one in the family with strong passions. I heard many debates between relatives and friends that got very loud as each person stood their ground on an issue. No one in our family considered these fights mean-spirited, and no one was uncomfortable; we just saw them as being strong in what you believed in. If you discovered you were wrong, it was acceptable to change your mind because someone made a better argument. I learned to be strong and not be wishy-washy. If you're wrong, change; and if you're right, help others see it your way.

Now, I admit, with all those strong personalities it was hard to see where kindness fit in, but it did. Everyone in my family would give anyone else a shirt, a meal, or money if they needed it. Nearly every day of my life I watched my parents open their door to complete strangers. And because we lived in the woods a good ways out of town, we were also the recipients of kindness. If one of us was sick or needed anything, the people in our church and community would come to help us.

These qualities help me in all areas of life today. For me, running a company, especially with most of my family on the payroll, demands both strength and kindness. I have to stay strong in making decisions that are best for our company, and I have to be strong to withstand the worries that come with owning a business.

But I also need to be kind—otherwise, no one will want to work for me. There have been times when I've taken grown men to the mall and bought them new clothes in a sort of redneck makeover. I've arranged transportation to help others get to work, helped people get a date—can you say Duck Commander Dating Service?—or simply worked with them to boost their confidence. I've never been a fan of people being mistreated in any way.

Korie and I work together every day. This can be a challenge because when you're in the workplace together and then go home together, it can really test your kindness. We like to use our strength to treat each other with kindness. We've seen some great, strong marriages be able to do it. It can be done.

Like Korie, I value these two traits and work hard to instill them in our children. I'm very blessed to have a partner like Korie, who is a strong and kind woman of God. I have no doubt that our children will learn these two traits by watching her as she raises them to love God and each other. This is her book, but I've got a few things to say along the way. I hope you enjoy it and get something out of it that will help you raise your kids to be strong and kind too.

PART ONE

THE IMPORTANCE OF
GOOD CHARACTER

YOU'VE GOT THIS

I'm so excited to be on this parenting journey with you. It's the most challenging job we will ever have but by far the most rewarding. God gave those little munchkins to you—to teach, inspire, discipline, learn from, laugh with, cheer on, bandage up, dance with, and love without question or condition. You can do it. You've got this.

Throughout this book we will look at what it means to have good character. We'll delve deeper into many significant character traits. You will choose which ones you want to focus on in your family, and then we'll look at practical ways to instill these traits in your children.

But first I want you to know this: you are equipped for this task—this challenge of raising children with good values who will contribute in a positive way to this world. You get to decide how you want to raise them, what values you hold dear and want to pass along to them. They are your children, and you can't really go wrong when choosing, so don't stress about this part. The world needs strong and kind kids and patient and loving kids; we need kids with endurance and selflessness and those who are joyful and compassionate. Our world will certainly be a better place with kids who are disciplined and forgiving and those who are self-controlled and peaceful. What do you want to see in your children?

At the end of this book I'm going to ask you to choose any two traits, but this isn't a test. God has given us a wide pasture in which to graze and live as His children. We are free in Him, and you are free to choose which traits you want for your children.

After the choosing is where the hard part comes in, however. Once you determine the traits that are important to your family, then you have to live like it. You can't pick courage and then not allow your kids to walk out the door for fear something bad will happen to them. If you want your kids to be courageous, you have to live courageously, even if you're scared. It doesn't do much good to talk about it but then turn around and live the opposite. Kids see right through that.

In this book you will see that Willie and I certainly aren't perfect parents, but we are, like you, striving to raise children with good values, who contribute positively to this world, and who most importantly love God and love others. And that pretty much sums it up.

ONE

THE CHARACTER CHALLENGE

Society suffers when children are not taught good values and morals, and I believe we are seeing that play out in our country today. Studies show that most American parents are concerned about the moral decline of future generations, and they have a right to be. A "survey of two thousand American adults . . . reveals a strong majority, 74 percent, believes moral values in America are weaker than they were twenty years ago. Almost half, 48 percent, [believe] that values are much weaker than they were twenty years ago."[1]

It's also interesting to note that almost two-thirds of those surveyed said the media is an important factor in our culture, and 68 percent said that the media's effect on the country's moral values is a negative one.[2] No argument here. For a long time, television has focused on characters rather than on people with character. There's a big difference.

SHOWING GOOD CHARACTER

I know, our family is contributing to this media culture. The importance of our showing good character rather than simply being good characters is not lost on us. From the first day of filming *Duck Dynasty*, we felt a little push to be what the television world considers good "characters"—to argue more, to be unkind to our spouses, and for our kids to be disrespectful to us and to roll their eyes at their grandparents. Not that anyone tried to change our beliefs or cut the prayer at the end of our show, as some have reported, but the model that was supposed to work on reality television included showing people who fought—a lot—and cheated on their spouses, kids who lied and talked back to their parents, and young people who drank and partied. Reality shows are notorious for characters seeking their fifteen minutes of fame. People on the covers of magazines are the ones whose moral character is so often far from what most parents would want for their children.

Ever since the decline of shows such as *The Andy Griffith Show* and *The Waltons*, I believe people have been longing for a show that features people who strive to have good character, who love and forgive one another, who stick together as a family through thick and thin, and who have faith in something greater than themselves. I think that the more than twelve million people who watched the *Duck Dynasty* episode where Phil and Miss Kay renewed their vows proved that's exactly what America was looking for. Our family is certainly not perfect, but nobody wants to see people who are perfect. It's not realistic. We all have good and bad traits, times when we don't do what we should or when we behave in ways that aren't exactly how we would have hoped to behave. But *Duck Dynasty* has proven that a show in which people are striving to live good, moral lives can be successful in television today. In recent years we have seen a major increase in films about faith and family values, and some have been amazingly successful. It seems that Hollywood has taken note.

Surprisingly to him, although perhaps not so much to everyone else, Uncle Si has become the favorite by far on our show. The most common question I get when traveling around the country is, "Why didn't you bring Si with you?" As if it would be totally normal to travel with your crazy uncle everywhere you go! He certainly is a good character; he's funny, will do pretty much anything, has an iced-tea addiction, sports a straggly, salt-and-pepper (well, more salt than pepper) beard, and is missing a few teeth. He *is* a character! But beyond that, and perhaps what is at the root of people's love for him, is that Uncle Si is a man of good character. He loves his family, his country, and God. He's also a gentleman who treats his family respectfully, is benevolent to others, and is kind. That isn't an apt description of many celebrities today. Sadly, in modern America we more often cheer for one who is an over-the-top character rather than one who has good character.

A CHALLENGE TO TODAY'S TEENAGERS

Statistics tell us that teens today are acting out in ways our grand-parents would never have imagined, resorting to drugs, alcohol, and self-destructive behaviors in staggering numbers. According to Samir Parikh, the director of mental health and behavioral sciences at Fortis Hospital in New Delhi, India, suicide was the second leading cause of death among fifteen- to twenty-nine-year-olds globally in 2012.[3] This shocking and sad statistic may hit close to home for some of you reading this book. I won't claim that what's written in this book will solve all of these problems, but I do think that by working to instill character in our children and, more importantly, put God back in His rightful place in our lives and our homes, we're setting the stage for a brighter future.

Before we move on, though, I don't want to paint the picture that all youth today are lacking in character. I have been more encouraged than ever from meeting young people doing some truly amazing things. Along with the moral decline that has clearly happened in our country, there seems to be an uprising of teens and twentysomethings who have a burning desire to do something meaningful with their lives and in the world. They want to make a difference in the lives of the less fortunate and to leave the world a better place than they found it. John Luke and Sadie speak all over the country and come back with incredible stories of how God is using young people to make a difference in their communi-ties and in the world.

For too long we've excused teenagers with an attitude of, "What can you expect out of them; they're just teenagers," or "They're just sow-ing their wild oats." By doing this, we are allowing them to miss out on all the benefits youth has to offer. Young people aren't as afraid to take risks, they are more open to new ideas, and they have tons of energy and more free time than they will have at any other time in their lives. Let's not write them off or make excuses for their youth. Let's challenge our teenagers to be people of character and leaders in their communities and the world. First Timothy 4:12 says, "Don't let anyone look down on you because you are young, but set an example for the believers in speech, in conduct, in love, in faith and in purity." I'm proud to say that our kids set an example for us daily!

What Is Character?

So let's take a look at what character really is. One definition of *character* is related to the mental and moral strengths distinctive to an individual. Another definition tells us that character is the way someone thinks, feels, and behaves—his or her personality.

It seems that as a society we have become confused about what is honorable and what constitutes moral strength. To take it a step further, who do we look up to and what do we value in a person; who do we idolize and call heroes; who do we end up modeling our lives after? We make important moral decisions by whichever direction the popular winds are currently blowing, how Hollywood chooses to portray something, or what the current self-help guru says in his or her latest book. While every family is free to have its own compass about many issues, and no two families go about life in exactly the same way, it seems we all should be able to agree that our world would be a better place if people were honest, kind, compassionate, self-controlled . . . you get the idea. Our methods may be different, but our core convictions should be relatively the same. At one time in our country's history, character and convictions did not vary much from one household to the next. Teachers, grandparents, preachers, aunts, and uncles all pretty much agreed as to what was right or wrong behavior and how to teach it to their children. I'm not sure that's true anymore. Today, when it comes to behavior, adults themselves seem to be struggling to agree on what's good and bad. Many are too scared to speak up in the interest of being politically correct or not harming a child's self-esteem. Perhaps all of the focus on the media, child psychology, and conflicting parenting experts is causing us to not know what we believe anymore. This confusion and lack of confidence in our values are causing insecurity in our parenting and children who don't know how to behave or what to believe.

Willie and his brother Jase love to tell the story of when their older brother Alan and his friends were caught drinking and tearing up mailboxes along the street. Willie and Jase were hiding behind the bushes as they watched Phil whup the entire group—three licks with a belt for Al and each of his friends. As they tell it, Al was wearing the short workout shorts that were popular in the 1970s. Willie and Jase watched with wide eyes as Al and his friends got what was due. Not only was this entertaining to the younger brothers, but it was a powerful lesson about what would happen to them if they ever got drunk and tore up someone else's stuff. I think this kept Willie and Jase out of a lot of trouble. The remarkable thing about this story is that every one of Alan's friends' parents thanked Phil for disciplining their boys when they needed it. We all know this would likely never happen in today's society. I'm not saying that it should; there are other ways to discipline teenagers (although, arguably, this method was effective, if not for Al, then for the two boys watching from the bushes). But the point is that one generation ago, everyone generally agreed on what was right and wrong and welcomed help from other parents in disciplining their children when they caught them misbehaving. Most parents today would be more likely to defend their child than to use the opportunity to teach them right from wrong.

Is it any wonder that children today are confused?

In our family we take character seriously. For instance, we have a zero-tolerance rule when it comes to being rude to any adult. Back talk is never permitted. Talking back to an adult can sometimes seem cute, or at least excusable, in a two-year-old. When a dad says it's time to go and the little toddler waves her hand and says, "No, Daddy," we tend to giggle and move on. But this is not nearly as cute from a twelve-year-old.

When John Luke was about two or three, he actually kicked his great-granddad. He was in a bad mood for who knows why—probably Sadie had done something to get on his nerves. So while Papaw Shack was trying to help him get in the car, our sweet firstborn, John Luke, hauled off and kicked him! I was mortified. This was certainly not accepted behavior in our home, and John Luke knew by my swift reaction that he'd better not ever try that again. I tell you this to say that just because we don't allow something doesn't mean our kids will never do it; it just means we need to work to teach them what's acceptable and what's not. And if no adult ever tells them or disciplines them when they do something like kick their great-granddad, stick their tongue out at an adult, or give their mom a little sass, how will they ever learn?

My advice is, don't tolerate bad behavior at age two, and you won't have to deal with it at twelve. I'm pretty sure that "no back talk to adults" used to be a rule in every household, and everyone agreed that no child would be allowed to speak to an adult in a rude manner. It was common for adults to correct the manners of children within their realm of influence. The child's parents would be thankful for the help in teaching their child. Today, if you corrected another child's manners, even a child of a friend or family member, the parent might just tell you off, or at least look at you as if you were crazy. But in our family, when one of our nieces or nephews answers an adult with a "Yeah," it's totally expected and accepted to hear that adult correct them: "Yes, ma'am." We value good manners in our children and are happy when other adults who know and love our children help teach them.

However, today our children no longer have the good fortune of knowing that every adult will stand together to ensure they reach adulthood with good manners and good character. Sadly, children can be heard in restaurants, on school campuses, and at Disney World speaking unkindly to their parents while the parents do nothing about it. Many parents seem content to allow their children to talk to them in any way they want. Parents even argue regularly with their kids. This does not teach children to respect adults or people in authority, and it will set them up for difficulties in school, on their sports teams, and, as adults, in their jobs or other areas where they must be respectful of authority figures. Children who talk back and constantly argue with their parents keep their home from being the peaceful place it was meant to be.

Character Is a Big Deal

George Barna is the founder of the Barna Group. You may not have heard of him, but his research on the intersection of faith and culture is very insightful. If you've ever wondered where preachers get all those numbers and facts they quote on Sundays, well, this is the guy behind all the research. In his book *Revolutionary Parenting*, Barna identifies a list of character traits most people believe are critical to the successful development of children. He reported that 100 percent of the parent groups he surveyed for his book felt that the most important focus of their children's training was the development of godly character.[4] One hundred percent! It's hard to argue with that statistic. Character *is* a big deal.

Dr. Thomas Lickona, developmental psychologist and professor of education at the State University of New York at Cortland, has won awards in character education and is currently the director of the Center for the Fourth and Fifth Rs (Respect and Responsibility). This center is all about teaching children character.

According to Dr. Lickona, virtues are objectively good because they

- affirm our human dignity,
- promote the well-being and happiness of the individual,
- serve the common good,
- define our rights and obligations, and
- meet the classical ethical tests of reversibility (would you want to

be treated this way?) and universalizability (would you want all persons to act this way in a similar situation?).[5]

Look closely at that last point. It sounds like what we call the Golden Rule: "Do unto others as you would have them do unto you." The Golden Rule is based on the principle Jesus taught in Matthew 7:12: "In everything, do to others what you would have them do to you, for this sums up the Law and the Prophets."

This verse is the heart of Christianity. Later in the Bible, Jesus says it this way:

> Jesus replied: "'Love the Lord your God with all your heart and with all your soul and with all your mind.' This is the first and greatest commandment. And the second is like it: 'Love your neighbor as yourself.' All the Law and the Prophets hang on these two commandments." (Matt. 22:37–40)

Can you imagine what a different world we would live in if we all did that? God, in His infinite wisdom, knows that loving Him and loving others is the key to a happy life.

My dad has an interesting twist on the Golden Rule. He says that instead of treating others as you would treat yourself, you should treat others as they want to be treated. His logic is that others may not want or need the same thing you want or need, so look carefully and try to meet the needs of the other person. He makes a valid point.

OUR RESPONSIBILITY AS PARENTS

Our value system and our good character traits set the standard for our actions and attitudes, which ultimately shape who we are, how we live, and how we treat others. But those value systems are being challenged.

Are these challenges and changes to be blamed on those pervasive societal influencers mentioned earlier, such as media, peer pressure, and other outside influences on our children? According to a special report by the Culture and Media Institute, of the American adults who say that young people today have a weaker sense of right and wrong than young people did twenty years ago, 21 percent blame media, while 57 percent blame parents and families.[6] It is significant to note that over half of those surveyed believe we, the parents, are to blame.

Parents, we are gatekeepers for our children when it comes to their exposure to the media, friends, and outside influences. We must be the ones guiding our children, instilling in them good values and character traits. When asked what virtues are important, respondents to the survey I mentioned earlier indicated that Americans most value truthfulness, thrift, industry, and charity. However, when it comes to living out these virtues, we aren't exactly living up to the standards we hold. One-fourth of the participants in this survey "admitted they would cheat on restaurant checks, tax returns, and breaking laws they considered outdated or if no one gets hurt."[7]

What America needs today is parents who don't just say they value these virtues but who live them and passionately and boldly teach them to their children. It's up to me and you and every parent in America to make the necessary changes to give our children the opportunity to change the world. We do that by instilling good character traits in them so that they will be capable of being the adults our world needs.

TWO

CHARACTER AND THE BIBLE

I was the children's minister at our church for several years when our children were babies and toddlers. We spent a lot of time in our classes, talking about the characters written about in the Bible. We told stories of people such as Adam and Eve, Cain and Abel, Noah, Moses, Jonah, and David. There were also Esther, Rahab, Hannah, Solomon, Abraham and Sarah, Naomi, Jacob and Esau, Mary and Martha, Mary and Joseph, and others—all with real lives that taught our kids about God, how He cares for us and loves us. Their lives also teach us godly values and principles, as well as lessons on character.

We know our character is reflected in our behavior. You can't say that someone has good character when his or her actions prove the opposite. This doesn't mean we won't make mistakes. All these people in the Bible had moments when they exhibited strong, positive character traits, but they also had times when they missed the mark, when they failed. Even the apostle Paul, who was a great man of God and wrote much of the New Testament, talks in Romans 7 about doing what he doesn't want to do rather than what he wants to do.

> I do not understand what I do. . . . For I have the desire to do what is good, but I cannot carry it out. For I do not do the good I want to do, but the evil I do not want to do—this I keep on doing. Now if I do what I do not want to do, it is no longer I who do it, but it is sin living in me that does it. . . . Who will rescue me from this body that is subject to

death? Thanks be to God, who delivers me through Jesus Christ our Lord! (vv. 15, 18–20, 24–25)

This is the struggle of every person. We all need God's great love for us to rescue us through the blood of Jesus Christ. So please don't misunderstand me—a person of good character is not perfect. We are human, and with that come temptation and failure. We all are in need of God's unconditional love and perfect sacrifice of Jesus.

Let's look closely at the Bible to see what it says about good character and why it's important.

Good Character Produces a Good Life

> My son, do not forget my teaching,
>   but keep my commands in your heart,
> for they will prolong your life many years
>   and bring you peace and prosperity. (Prov. 3:1–2)

I would imagine this is the wish of all parents: for our children to have long lives full of peace and prosperity. This proverb tells us how to get it by keeping God's commands in our hearts. Continuing on to verses 5 and 6, we read, "Trust in the LORD with all your heart / and lean not on your own understanding; / in all your ways submit to him, / and he will make your paths straight." I don't believe what God is describing is a boring life with the perfect yard, white house, and picket fence. He is offering a life of confidence, an assurance that He has gone before us to smooth out and straighten the path. God offers lives without all the bumps in the road that we bring upon ourselves when we take our eyes off of Him, think we've got it all figured out, and forget to follow His teaching.

When the children were still quite young, we spent a long weekend at our church's family camp. We'd had a great time doing crafts, playing games, singing and dancing, and learning about God with our kiddos, but on the last day, Willie had to leave early to get back to work. That left me to pack up our sleeping bags, clothes, snacks, crafts, and our four kids, all under the age of seven . . . alone. By the time I got us all into the minivan, I was exhausted and not feeling all that holy anymore. We were driving home, down a little country road, and the kids were obviously feeling the same way I was feeling about life—grouchy. They were fussing and fighting while I was trying to control the chaos from the driver's seat.

That's when it happened. Sadie spilled an entire box of Nerds candy in the backseat! Who gave my kid Nerds? (That was when our family's ban on Nerds was enacted. From then on, no one was allowed to eat Nerds ever again!) I was looking back to see what had happened, griping to the kids about whatever caused the big spill, when I heard a sound that sent my heart racing. A siren. And I had foolishly thought that this day couldn't get any worse.

I pulled over to the side of the road, and the police officer asked me to please step out of the car. He politely asked me if I was feeling okay. "Yes, sir," I replied. He went on to tell me that he had been behind me for a while now and I was swerving all over the road. That was when I realized what he was insinuating. My eyes were brimming with tears as I told him that I was sorry I had been swerving but that I had kids arguing in the car and one had spilled Nerds all over the backseat.

He said, "Ma'am, would you like me to talk to them? I can put a little fear into those kids if you want me to." Why in the world I didn't let him do it, I will never know. It would have been a much better story if I had taken him up on that offer and one that the kids would never have forgotten. Instead, my pride wouldn't let me let him do it. "No sir, I've got it under control," I told him, even though I really didn't feel in control at the moment—I felt totally outnumbered. I promised I would keep an eye on the road and there would be no more problems. He was nice enough to let me off the hook with a warning. On that day our path was not all that straight. I was swerving all over the road. I foolishly thought I was in control, when really I was anything but. I got back in the car and calmly explained to the little faces staring at me what had just happened. Then

I started driving again, this time talking to God, asking him to grant me patience and wisdom, and I kept my hands on the steering wheel and my eyes on the road.

Have you noticed that when you get away from God's plan, life becomes anything but peaceful? Your path gets bumpy and dark? There's a reason for that: it's not God's plan for your life! It isn't that God is mean; it's that God is *right*. He knows what it takes to live peacefully on earth, and He gave us His Word to share that information with us. When we choose not to follow it, we tend to swerve all over the road.

GOOD CHARACTER PRODUCES BEHAVIOR LIKE GOD'S

> He has shown you, O mortal, what is good.
> And what does the LORD require of you?
> To act justly and to love mercy
> and to walk humbly with your God. (Micah 6:8)

It is possible for someone to have morals, strong convictions about right and wrong, and good character traits without knowing God. Being a good person does not depend on believing Jesus' good news. By the same token, a person who claims to follow God is not guaranteed to display good character. I believe that a moral code has been written on our hearts by our Creator. But whether you believe God is the source of all good in the world or not, living by a moral code is important for society to function. I would venture to guess that if you took a poll of character traits people value, you would find that most people agree on most of them, such as honesty and kindness. When we choose to follow an ethical code of conduct, our rights and obligations are clearly marked—that's our boundary.

Boundaries are a good thing. Boundaries say, "You're protected as long as you stay within these confines." As we grow, our boundaries move and change in appearance, but the reason for them remains the same—protection. Eventually, if we've been taught to abide by and appreciate boundaries, we're able to set them for ourselves. We can say no when no is the answer that will protect us. Saying no is a type of boundary, as is a fence or a crib; it provides a hedge of protection. Adhering to a code of good behavior means that there is no question about what we should do when we are confronted with a choice. God doesn't have to be in the picture for this to happen, but nonetheless, such behavior is godlike, which means everyone wins.

Many of God's laws are universal. The Bible tells us that when Jesus came, He fulfilled the law. The Spirit now lives in us, and His law is written on our hearts. In the Bible the apostle Paul explains it this way:

> You show that you are a letter from Christ, the result of our ministry, written not with ink but with the Spirit of the living God, not on tablets of stone but on tablets of human hearts.
>
> Such confidence we have through Christ before God. Not that we are competent in ourselves to claim anything for ourselves, but our competence comes from God. He has made us competent as ministers of a new covenant—not of the letter but of the Spirit; for the letter kills, but the Spirit gives life. (2 Cor. 3:3–6)

Our goal as Christians is to become more and more like God, not by trying to follow the letter of the law perfectly but by allowing His Spirit to live in us—to become more like Him as we seek to know and love Him. We want to take on His traits. As we teach our children to have the character of God, we are helping them find their way to heaven while also helping them to live the best possible life while on this earth.

Some of my proudest moments as a parent have been when someone told me something good our children did that I didn't even know they were doing. Commend your children when they do good things; catch them doing good, and let them know that those are the things you value. So often our children are praised for achievements such as getting good grades or being the star athlete, but kindnesses, such as stopping to pull someone out of a ditch, being a friend to the new kid at school, or noticing when an older person needs help and pitching in without being asked, sometimes go unnoticed. People have told me that our kids have done all of these things at one time or another; that's when I know we've done okay as parents.

Willie's mom, Miss Kay, will be the first to tell you that she's a slow walker. The rest of the family walks rather quickly, especially now that our pictures are on T-shirts and billboards. If we walk slowly, we might never make it through the airport. We all take turns staying back with Miss Kay, but she's extra thankful when one of our children notices her in the back of the group and keeps her company as she walks. At some point all of our kids have done this without being asked, and Miss Kay always lets me know how much she appreciates their thoughtfulness.

Once, we were in Baton Rouge for a state track meet in which John Luke, Sadie, and Reed, Jase and Missy's oldest son, were competing. We had a little time between events, so some of the family decided to go exploring while I stayed behind with the team. The family saw a trolley passing by and decided to jump on to go see another part of the campus. Miss Kay told me later that Bella noticed that she wasn't going to make it, so Bella quickly ran back to be with her, knowing she'd miss the trolley but not wanting her Mamaw Kay to be left alone. Jesus asks us to do for others as we would want them to do for us, which is exactly what Bella did in that moment. She got just as much praise that day as did the teens who won the state track championship.

THREE

MAKE SURE YOU
RUN THE SHOW

My grandparents were born too late to officially qualify as part of the "greatest generation" (1901–1921), but I was fortunate enough to spend lots of time with them growing up, and I'm here to testify to their greatness. They were children during the Great Depression and World War II. Children raised during such times didn't have the luxury of being the center of anyone's world. This may be one secret to their greatness.

Values of the Greatest Generation

My grandparents on both sides of my family came from large families with few material possessions. Their parents struggled to put food on the table. They wanted to leave this world a better place than it was when they got here, and through hard work and determination, they did just that. Both sets of grandparents started their own businesses and were active in many nonprofits. Their funerals were celebrations joined by more than a thousand people whose lives had been touched by their wisdom, love, and support. I believe we have much to learn from past generations.

My grandparents lived through the Great Depression, breadlines, World War II, and the Korean War. Living through just one of those events would be enough to teach them what is truly important in life, but my grandparents, and maybe yours, lived through all of these. Anyone who has experienced tough times knows that shared difficulties bind people together in a way that good times seldom do. Unfortunately the times of prosperity in America today seem to be a breeding ground for selfish behavior. We may have to work harder to combat this, but it's worth the extra effort.

During my grandparents' day, even in their leisure time, the focus was on the whole family. My grandpa on my dad's side could play any instrument, and so could his brothers. When I was a little girl, I loved watching them play music together, but it wasn't until I was older that I realized how significant it was. Do you think that my grandfather's parents worried about whether their children would learn to play an instrument? Or that they spent money sending him and his brothers to music lessons? Or to band camp? No. That was a luxury they couldn't afford. What they did do was gather the family together on the weekends for some "pickin' and grinnin'," as they called it. Times were hard, but families still found ways to bond and have fun. If you wanted to join the family band, you were expected to find a guitar, piano, or banjo during the week and figure it out. No one would sit beside you to make sure you practiced thirty minutes a day. No one had time. They were too busy tending to the farm and trying to keep food on the table.

My Papaw Shack, on my mother's side, had five brothers and one sister. Their father was an alcoholic who left home when my grandfather was a teenager. One brother was killed in a motorcycle accident at age sixteen, but five of the six remaining children graduated from college without any financial help from their single mom, who worked hard to put food on the table. As adults, they all held jobs of great importance in their communities; they were political officials and church leaders. I'm privileged to see pictures of my hardworking little great-grandmother, the mother of my Papaw Shack, surrounded by her grown sons, all proudly wearing their military uniforms. At family reunions, they would sit around the table and tell stories from the good ol' days. Those days seemed pretty difficult to me, but now I understand that those hard times built some mighty men and women. Yes, there is much to learn from past generations who kept their focus not on individual members but on the family as a whole and on their faith.

From all indications a child-centered society is a rather new development. For centuries children were likely to be told, "Children are to be seen and not heard." Today, children are not only seen, but they are the ones being asked where or what they want to eat for dinner and even more important questions, like whether Mommy and Daddy should have another child or move into a new house. Children have been given a loud voice, and they use that voice with no reservations. As I already mentioned, America's past is replete with hard times, and when times are hard, childhood is shortened. Papaw Shack would tell of cleaning the school building when he was eight years old for a few pennies and nickels to help support his family. Such stories are not unusual. Neither was it unusual for children to eat everything on their plate, because that was all they were going to get.

As our society has grown wealthier, the treatment of children has improved. Thankfully, we have child labor laws that protect them from being used or harmed in the workplace, and truancy laws ensure that all children are educated. I can't even imagine my eight-year-old heading out each morning to clean the bathrooms at school. I'm grateful that our children today are protected from such mistreatment. But as is typical, the pendulum may have swung too far in the other direction.

PEOPLE ARE MORE IMPORTANT THAN THINGS

Family is our first look at behavior in a community. To quote my dad, it's where we should learn "to share and to care" about others. Before every evening meal he would pray that we all "share and care" more each day. It may seem like a small thing, but if we would resolve to share and care more, how much better would our world be? Ideally, we learn how to behave at home and then carry those lessons out into the bigger world. But today's families are often split by divorce or even split within homes. By that I mean that in many homes, every child has his or her own room, cell phone, TV, set of toys, and group of friends. What previous generations learned through experience must be taught deliberately in America today.

Back when a household had only one phone, one television set, and one bathroom, sharing wasn't an option; it was a necessity. Children learned how to get along with others, respect the property of others, and be grateful for what they had as part of daily life for countless generations past, but not so today. Willie and I don't allow televisions in our children's bedrooms; however, they do have their own rooms and their own cell phones. Yes, this is America in 2015, and we all live in it. But nothing makes me happier than hearing Sadie and Bella giggling in the bed together as they go to sleep. I love that they want to be together instead of locking each other out of their rooms. We strive to be conscious of the fact that we have plenty and that what we have is a gift to be used wisely and shared generously.

My grandmother says that no one thing is more important than a person's feelings. Our Howard Family Legacy of Principles for Living (listed in the appendix) states that "people are more important than things." I can't tell you how many times I've quoted this to our children when they've come tattling that someone has broken their favorite toy or is blocking their view of the television. This phrase was on repeat in our home during my kids' younger years, and I hope it has sunk in. We strive to keep "things" in their proper place and never let them become more valuable than people.

The Importance of Family over a Single Child

Willie and I have also been deliberate about keeping family, not any single child, first. When our children were young, we did this by not allowing one child's bad mood to ruin the peacefulness of the home for the rest of us. As my grandmother used to say, "You may stay, but your bad attitude may not." I tended to put it a little more bluntly: "If you're going to act like that, go to your room." Even when our children were very young, if they woke up from a nap on the wrong side of the bed, as the saying goes, then they had the opportunity to spend a little more time in said bed until they were able to find the other side. We didn't allow screaming and throwing fits to ruin everyone else's day. When our kids behaved that way, they were simply asked to go back to their rooms until they could come out and be pleasant.

We taught our children the importance of family over a single child in other ways too. For example, when Sadie was on *Dancing with the Stars*, we made sure it was a family experience. Our entire family—including cousins, aunts, uncles, grandparents, and siblings—flew out to California to share in this experience. Sadie's victory wasn't hers alone; it was everyone's. And we are grateful that *Duck Dynasty* is about our entire family and not just one of us.

Please realize that you don't have to be a celebrity family to be affected by the current child-centered phenomenon. Many families today rearrange the entire family's schedule to accommodate a budding athlete or musician. I don't mean that you shouldn't nurture and affirm those talents—of course you should. The problem isn't nurturing the child; it's holding that child's talent and schedule as having more importance than those of other family members or the family as a whole.

The Me Generation

There is much debate today about the me generation. Here's my two cents' worth on that: we were all me-kids. It is human nature to first want what pleases you. But someone, hopefully your mom and dad, should see to it that *me* is soon replaced by *we*. Me-kids don't get that way without their parents' help in supporting that agenda, and every child has the potential to be the "me, me, me" child. If you've ever had a two-year-old, you know that *me* and *mine* are two of their favorite words. But strong, kind, loving parents who are leaders begin the process of teaching that two-year-old that the world does not revolve around him or her and that to cope in this world, he or she will need to start looking at others as the gateway to a happier life. Sadly, in my opinion, we've lost our way a bit in this arena. It's time to bring our families back to focusing on families rather than on the individuals who occupy the same space for a few short years.

A recent study confirms that narcissists (self-centered people) are largely bred, not born. The study found that narcissism in children is cultivated by parental overvaluation: parents believing their child to be more special and more entitled than others.[1] The good news is that if well-meaning parents have created this problem, the same parents can fix it. Many of the things we are talking about in this book will help you raise children who are not narcissists. Treating others with kindness, learning manners, showing unconditional love, not giving constant approval, teaching the value of hard work, and putting others before self are all great steps toward remedying the present condition of many—young and old alike.

We're given this warning in Philippians 2:3: "Do nothing out of selfish ambition or vain conceit. Rather, in humility value others above yourselves." Suffice it to say that Paul recognized the problem many years ago. It seems that the me generation has always existed. As Christian parents, we have to do our part to turn around that me-train and help our children see that others are just as important as themselves.

FOUR

LET YOUR CHILDREN GROW UP

Our family has been involved with Christian camps for many years. The camp we love and support hosts between one and two hundred campers each week. When registering, each camper is allowed to pick one bunkmate or friend to be in the cabin with him or her. One year a young mother arrived at the camp late on check-in day and had not filled out that part of the registration form. By the time she and her daughter arrived, the cabins were all assigned and most of the bunks were already taken. This meant her child would have to take whatever bunk was left and sleep beside someone she didn't know. This could have been a great learning opportunity, the mom assuring her daughter that it would be fine, she would have a great week meeting new friends and, at the end of the week, she would be eager to hear the stories of all the new kids her daughter had met. The conversation never occurred. Instead, the young mom opened her purse and offered the child in the bed next to her child ten dollars if she would give up her bunk so her child's friend could sleep there. Not what I was expecting! But it happens all too often these days as parents do everything they can to ensure their child's happiness. They'll pay off anyone necessary to make sure that all is right in their precious child's world.

Parents' overinvolvement in their children's lives is another factor contributing to the general decline of moral strength and character. We have convinced ourselves that our children always need help. Our heads know this isn't true, but our hearts struggle with the idea of leaving our kids alone.

Perhaps we can keep this in perspective when we realize that just a few generations ago, children were working, cooking, and taking care of a home at ages when our children can barely tie their shoes. As a matter of fact, in the early 1900s, the word *teenager* didn't even exist. You were a child, and then you were an adult; there was no in-between. The word *teenager* was first used sometime between 1934 and 1961. It didn't appear in *Webster's Dictionary* until the third edition, which came out in 1961.[1]

What Makes a Child-Centric Home?

I can think of a couple of factors that contribute to the problem of child-centric homes; you can probably add others.

Fewer Children in the Family

First, the number of children per household is lower today than at any other time in modern history. It just makes sense that a mom with six children is not as likely to hover as a mom with two. She simply doesn't have time. When there are more children in the family, the older children have to pitch in to help, and the younger kids have to become independent faster—they have to learn to do things for themselves. I'm not telling you to have more kids, but it's good to be aware that in today's smaller families, it's much easier for parents to give extra attention to the one or two children they have in the home.

Parents in Love with Their Kids

Another factor contributing to the problem of child-centric homes is that modern Americans seem to be *in love* with their kids—seriously, *in* love and infatuated. Look at the bumper stickers in the parking lot at the grocery store, and you'll be barraged with competing claims to the neighborhood's greatest kids. I love my children with all my heart and soul, but I'm in love with their daddy, not with them. That's a big distinction. When Willie and I do our job right, our children will grow up, fall in love with someone, get married, and go off to live their own lives. They'll still love us, of course, but they won't be in love with us. Meanwhile, Willie and I will still be together, holding hands, and as much in love as the day we said, "I do." That's the plan and the goal. When we're in love with our children instead of with our spouse, things can get all twisted around and messed up, and families start falling apart. One small example of this is the way Valentine's Day has been hijacked by our children. I have grudgingly participated, year after year, in elaborate Valentine's Day parties at school for kids because somehow they have become the norm, but I've never understood them. Thankfully, all of my kids are in middle school or beyond now, so there are no more silly Valentine's Day parties to go to. My husband is my valentine, and our children should know that. If they don't, it's time we started showing them.

Protecting Kids from Disappointment

Most families probably aren't aware of the problems that develop when parents create homes that revolve around the children and when they always run interference for their children. I recently read an article that said psychologists today are seeing increasing numbers of twenty-somethings who are depressed and don't know why. One observation and conclusion is that many of these children have experienced no major disappointments in their lives, so when they reach their twenties and normal disappointments occur, they don't know how to handle them.[2]

In her book *The Blessing of a Skinned Knee*, Dr. Wendy Mogel suggests that when we insulate children from difficult situations, we don't equip them to deal with adversity later in life. According to Dr. Mogel, college deans are reporting more "teacups," incoming freshmen who are too fragile to handle life away from home.[3] I've read several variations of this truth, but the bottom line is that parents today spend too much time preparing the road for their children instead of their children for the road. No parent is happy when a child is hurt (emotionally or physically), but if we don't go back to approaching hurts as life lessons rather than feeling guilty for not stopping them from happening, we're setting up our children for failure.

James 1:2–4 says, "Consider it pure joy, my brothers and sisters, whenever you face trials of many kinds, because you know that the testing of your faith produces perseverance. Let perseverance finish its work so that you may be mature and complete, not lacking anything." When we take away all of the trials and disappointments from our children's lives, we're robbing them of the opportunity to develop perseverance and the ability to become mature and complete human beings.

Constant Communication

Another thing that contributes to our tendency to overparent is all the modern inventions, including our cell phones. We're never more than a phone call away from anyone at any time. Today you can call, text, FaceTime, Skype, Snapchat, Viber—the list goes on and on—with a touch of your fingertip. But is this constant connection keeping us from allowing our children to grow up?

One of the most life-altering experiences Willie and I had as a young married couple was spending a semester studying in Italy. It was fun, exciting, and sometimes a bit scary. We were able to face events that included a terrorist attack, protest marches, and riding the train overnight under constant threat of being robbed. We also saw amazing historical sites and enjoyed staying in an Italian villa. Because Willie and I are both spontaneous and not great planners, we were lost most of the time, but we loved every minute. It was a great experience for us to have together as newlyweds. We weren't able to text or even e-mail our families back home because the age of social media and immediate contact with family members had not yet begun. Answering tough questions in our college courses, finding our way around a foreign country, and navigating through interactions with new friends and college professors were things we had to figure out on our own. We were barely nineteen and twenty, and we didn't have our parents or families one text, e-mail, FaceTime, or Instagram away. We called home once every week or two and chattered on and on about our adventures. Our parents expressed concern and joy, but at the end of the day, the journey was ours.

This seems absurd to our children today, and I admit, I love being able to see and hear about my children's experiences as they are going through them. We live in awesome times! Long distance hardly matters these days, as we get to be part of the lives of family members who live many miles from us. But in spite of this easy access, we must be able to step back and let our children experience life without our intervention. We must let them handle tough decisions and disappointments.

I like to hear from my kids while they are on a trip without me. Of course, I'm excited when they return home and want them to tell me all about it, but I'm not the one to call them often while they are away. I will check in every once in a while with a text, asking how they are doing, but generally, I feel if they need me, they will call. I didn't realize I was doing anything that special or different until John Luke came back from a school trip overseas. Before he began telling me about all of his adventures, he hugged me tightly and said, "Thanks, Mom, for being just how you are."

I smiled and said, "What's this about?"

He went on to explain, "All of the other moms are so overprotective. They call their kids nonstop, worrying about every little thing. Thank you for not being that way and for trusting me and letting me figure things out for myself."

Raising children like this may mean they make a few more mistakes. They may take the long road home sometimes or end up stuck in a ditch on the side of the road every once in a while. But in those times they'll gain something far greater than if a parent had solved their problem for them: they'll learn to become people with strong character.

TEN SIGNS OF OVERPROTECTIVE PARENTING

I recently read about a college professor who received a text from a mom asking whether her son had his coat on. I hope you're shaking your head at that one. But if you were thinking, *what a great idea,* you might be overprotective. Here's a list of ten things I have seen parents do that might be considered overprotective. How many of them sound like you?

1. When your child forgets his sporting equipment, homework assignment, or lunch for the fifth time, you still take the forgotten item to him one more time. (Mental reasoning you use to make yourself feel better—from now on referred to as MR: *He has such a busy schedule. How could he possibly remember all his stuff?*)

2. At mealtime you cook several choices so everyone is happy. (MR: *No one should go hungry, and I don't like everything either.*)

3. Every time your child misbehaves, you justify it by saying she is just tired. (MR: *My child didn't get her nap, so she shouldn't be required to be nice.*)

4. If your child is not invited to a party, you call to ask why. (MR: *That was just wrong. I have to look out for my child's self-esteem.*)

5. When your child's report card isn't up to par, instead of asking him why it isn't, you ask the teacher. (MR: *Surely the teacher made a mistake. My child would not lie to me about doing his homework.*)

6. If one sibling has a birthday, you make sure all siblings receive gifts. (MR: *It's never fair for one to get more than the others.*)

7. You are careful to not assign chores to your kids because they often have homework. (MR: *They have so much to do with school and all. Kids need to be kids.*)

8. If your child is not picked for the all-star team, you declare that politics were involved. (MR: *It's not possible that my offspring isn't talented enough. They always pick the coaches' sons.*)

9. At the end of the sports season, you volunteer to get trophies for all of the kids. (MR: *This is such a crucial time in their development, and all the kids played so hard.*)

10. When friends are coming to play, you put away the toys that your child doesn't like to share. (MR: *I'm an adult, and I don't like to share either, so why should she?*)

This list might be a little exaggerated to make a point, but the reality is that our generation is guilty as charged. As scary as it is, we have to let our children grow up, and growing up means they have to learn to do things for themselves. If you have a high school student in your household, prepare him to live life without you in his hip pocket. Don't answer every question for her. Don't fill out important documents for him. Don't drive her every place she needs to go. Don't make an appointment for him to get his hair cut and then call him to make sure he remembered to go.

I get it; it's hard! We love our kiddos! But we have to start preparing our kids for the road ahead, and that road is rarely as smooth as the road they travel while living with Mom and Dad.

FIVE

TO BEHAVE OR NOT TO BEHAVE

I remember the moment with each of our children when I could almost see this question pop into their little heads: *Does Mom mean business? Do I really have to do what Dad says*? It started pretty young, actually. John Luke was a climber. As a baby he would climb up me while I held on to him. As soon as he became mobile, he started climbing out of his bed and out of his high chair, and when he was barely able to walk, he pushed a chair over to the refrigerator and climbed on top. I'm not kidding! I found him sitting on top of our refrigerator before the age of two. He liked to test the limits; I would draw a line in the sand and tell him not to cross it, and then he would get as close as possible to that line. I could watch him deep in thought, contemplating what would happen if he stepped across it.

One day we were driving along and John Luke had been talking what seemed like incessantly: "Mom, what color is the sky?" "Mom, where are we going?" "Mom, can we go to the park?" "Mom, Mom, Mom . . ." I had reached my limit, so I said, "John Luke, do not say 'Mom' one more time for the rest of this trip." He sat quietly for a minute and said, "Korie?" I'm quite sure he thought he was minding me, but I knew I had some work to do.

Simply teaching our children to mind us or to behave will not solve all of our problems, but it is one piece of the puzzle. "Behave yourself" or "you need to behave" are probably two of the earliest phrases children hear. I know I've said those words to my kids plenty of times. But do we ever stop to tell our children what that phrase means, or do we just assume they get it because whatever they did was apparently *not* the right behavior?

APPROPRIATE BEHAVIOR IN VARIOUS SITUATIONS

I like this definition of *behave*: "to act in a certain manner to control yourself so your actions are acceptable and are considered appropriate by society."[1] We all must learn how to behave in our society, to act in a way that is appropriate for the situation. For instance, in church the appropriate behavior we ask of our children involves sitting as quietly as possible, bowing their heads during prayer, and singing along with the congregation. This is much easier for some kids than it is for others. It doesn't just happen naturally for most. Training from the parents is required to make this happen.

While running and playing is bad behavior during a church service, it's perfectly fine for a day at the beach. At the beach, bad behavior may involve whining and not sharing the sand toys. Teaching a child to behave appropriately in various settings involves training as well. To get the results you want, it's important to talk to your kids about what it means to behave in certain circumstances and what you expect of them. You can't expect kids to just know this. Trust me; they don't.

Many young parents think that teaching children to behave in various situations is too difficult, so they avoid going out in public for about four years of their child's life. We have five children, and each one came with a unique set of challenges. I'm here to tell you that while teaching good behavior might be difficult, it's not impossible.

As we talk about behavior and training children, I realize that there are children with special needs who require much different parenting tools and techniques. Children with special needs will benefit from all the things we are discussing, but the tools for those parents may be different from the ones used with a majority of children.

TRAIN UP A CHILD

When our children were toddlers, we began shaping their behavior. Notice that I said shaping, not controlling. One of the most popular Bible verses for parents is actually a proverb. Proverbs are truisms, not promises, but they contain great wisdom that we can apply to our lives. Proverbs 22:6 says, "*Train up a child* in the way he should go: and when he is old, he will not depart from it" (KJV). I really like the King James Version of this verse because of the word *train*. *Train* implies that this will take some time and plenty of effort. No one trains for a marathon only by running from the house to the mailbox. Training for a marathon takes consistent discipline, day after day, over many miles of running.

Training someone means teaching that person a particular skill or type of behavior. God is not being flippant about what He is asking us to do as parents. He doesn't say, "Let your child have some fun experiences in life, and hopefully he or she will also learn to be a good person." No, God uses a strong verb—*train*. He has charged you to *lead* your children to adulthood. *Leading* means showing them with words and actions.

So how did Willie and I train our children to behave in church? First, I packed a bag of toys, coloring books, and snacks. Little ones are too young to understand the sermon, so it's important to have something to keep their little minds entertained. When this didn't work and our children started misbehaving, throwing their toys on the floor and getting whiny or talking too loudly, Willie would take them to a quiet room and simply hold them. He wouldn't talk to them, play with them, or let them get down, no matter how much they squirmed. This sent them the message that if they misbehaved, they would be removed from the situation and taken to a safe environment where Dad had them, but they wouldn't be allowed to get what they wanted. Most of the time this produced big tears and lots of squirming, but Willie continued to hold them gently yet firmly until they calmed down and got the idea that they had better behave in church because what happened when they were taken out was not nearly as much fun.

GIVE YOUR CHILDREN TO GOD

Children are not new inventions. There have always been parents and children. Even before Adam and Eve had Cain and Abel, God had Adam and Eve; they were His children.

Parenting is not new, but it's also not easy. You would think that there would be clearly defined parameters for something so many centuries old; you would think mankind would have perfected it by now. But the simple truth is, we're human, and humans can pretty much make a mess out of anything.

We need training—but more important, we need God. At the end of the day, you have to give your children to God to complete. They belong ultimately to Him. He's the One who created them and the One who knows what is best for them.

SIX

SEE YOUR CHILDREN AS THE ADULTS YOU WANT THEM TO BE

It's often hard to look at our children when they're toddlers and see the men or women they will become. In fact, most of the time, we don't want to see that image. We want to enjoy our children as fun, free-spirited kids. When they're in the baby and toddler stages, I admit it's hard to see anything past changing diapers and keeping them fed. But as our children grow older, it is essential that we have a vision of the end goal. This has to happen to help children move from one stage to the next. Closing your eyes and visualizing your little man as the leader of his youth group or a Christian dad and your little girl as a mom or the president of a company will help you realize the importance of lovingly leading them toward these goals. This is how you prepare for a future with adult children who are pleasant to be around and who are contributing members of society.

LOOK AHEAD, THEN WORK BACKWARD

John Luke spoke recently at a teen conference where he challenged teens to start looking at the end of their life as a starting point. When we have a mental image of a goal, we're better able to accomplish that goal. John Luke told the teens that finding the best route from point A to point B is most often best realized by finding the route from B to A—working backward. He encouraged the teens to look ahead—not necessarily to *what* they want to be when they grow up, but *who* they want to be when they grow up. What kind of person, friend, parent, spouse, and worker do they want to be on this earth?

God actually created mankind in this way. He created Adam and Eve as grown adults. He saw His creation in its adult form, and then He worked backward. We must be able to see our children as adults if we are to start putting the traits in them today that we deem important for tomorrow.

Dieters have used this method for years. Many dieters will post a picture of themselves at their target weight on their refrigerator as an incentive to stick to the plan. Likewise, top athletes and successful business-people, in an attempt to be successful, often visualize themselves as having accomplished their goals before they even begin their journey.

In raising your children, you can apply this method in a couple of different ways. One is visualizing how you would like for them to be as adults and then prioritizing and teaching them those behaviors. Another way is purposefully fostering mentors, older children, or other adults in your children's lives who will be examples to your children. For example, Will loves music. He has a great voice and a talent for rapping and beat-boxing, so every chance we get, we try to put him in a position to talk to and hang out with Christians who are successful in that field. It's so much fun to see that light in your children's eyes when they begin to see how they could pursue their passion in life.

There is also nothing better than hearing that your children are examples and mentors for others. I got a text message the other day from a mom telling me that Will has been an example for her child. One of Will's gifts is making people feel special. From the time Will could talk, older ladies at church would tell me they love it when Will says hi to them and calls them by name. These are women I didn't even realize Will knew by name! One of my very best friends lives in Baton Rouge, and she says she loves it when she comes to visit because Will always makes her feel like she was missed and is loved.

Well, I got this text message from a mom of a five-year-old boy who is biracial like Will. She said she had been praying for godly examples her little boy could look up to who "look like him." That day Will had stopped in the hall at school and took the time to come over to her son and say hi to him and ask him how his day had gone. After Will walked away, she said to her son, "That was nice of Will to stop and talk to you." And her son replied, "Mom, he always checks on me and says hi to me." She said this was a clear answer to her prayers that God would provide good role models her son could relate to. She said, "In one sweet moment God showed me that He has this all through sweet Will!" Wow, that makes a mama's heart sing. I love that this mom was praying for her child and that Will was the answer to her prayer.

THE VALUE OF GOAL SETTING

Any type of goal setting has value. For one thing, it helps you separate what is relevant from what is not. Too often, we keep barking up the wrong tree in our quest for the right answers. Once you know how you want your children to be, you can relax and stop forcing them to be and do things that aren't relevant to their adult lives. In other words, you can stop sweating the small stuff. Parental goal setting also provides meaningful direction. Having a meaningful direction in life makes decisions faster and easier.

Willie has envisioned himself to be a lot of different things during our married life, and as you've probably noticed on *Duck Dynasty*, he doesn't do anything halfway. During our college years, he worked at the bowling alley and decided he might become a professional bowler. He played in several leagues, including a mixed-doubles one with me, and once bowled a 250, which is a really good game. He finally gave up the dream of professional bowling only to switch to Scrabble.

We were very competitive at Scrabble for a while. My family has had Scrabble tournaments most holidays for years, and we take it very seriously. Willie, however, got so serious that he studied the *Scrabble*

Dictionary. He learned every two-letter word in the dictionary, which is a huge asset when it comes to playing Scrabble. He learned so many obscure words, I couldn't tell if they were real or if he was just making them up. Then he decided he might go on the professional Scrabble circuit. Yes, that's a real thing! Well, once he realized there wasn't a lot of money to be made in professional Scrabble, he moved on to golf. I'm not sure he's given up his dream of becoming a professional golfer yet. As I write this, a full-fledged chipping practice is set up in our backyard, where you can find him most evenings.

For Willie, I think deciding he is going to go pro at something gives him a goal to work toward. It makes practice more fun to have a goal of becoming the best of the best, even if he never actually plays in the Masters one day.

At one point Willie and I saw ourselves as tennis players. Once we got a good picture of that in our heads, we took lessons and entered tournaments to achieve that goal. That was one of our small goals, and while we are not world-class tennis players, we do enjoy playing with our family and friends. When the desired end result is clear, we are far more likely to make better choices to reach that end. If you see your son as a dad who is capable of leading his family to the Lord, then you will easily make the choice to pay for him to attend a Christian camp or a leadership conference. If you see your daughter as a mom who lovingly leads her own daughters through life's trials, you won't succumb to the temptation to shield her from the issues she faces in her teen years.

Don't misunderstand me and think that parents are the molders and shapers of personalities. No, that's God's job. God is the one who gave our Rebecca her artistic side and her ability to laugh easily. He gave John Luke his spirit of adventure and love for the outdoors. He wired Will to love music and make friends easily. He gave Bella her quirky sense of humor and strong self-confidence. He put dancing in Sadie's DNA as well as her sensitive spirit. Parents have no control over those types of traits, and actually, the sooner we understand this, the easier our lives as parents will become.

Since we have both biological and adopted children in our family, it's easy to see the physical traits that are built into our children's DNA. With five children, whether they are biological or adopted, it's evident that God made each of them unique with individual talents, fears, strengths, and weaknesses.

Trying to force kids to be something they're not wired to be is like corralling a horse in a dog pen. Everyone will be miserable, because it just doesn't fit. Christians are often guilty of taking too much liberty with that often-quoted Bible verse that says, "I can do all things through Christ who strengthens me" (Phil. 4:13 NKJV). We would love for it to read, "Your children can do all things through Christ who strengthens them," as we proceed to shape the best baseball player, piano player, dancer, or gymnast who ever lived. Again, I am all for nurturing talent, but that verse in Philippians isn't talking about becoming the best opera singer or the next Michael Jordan. Remember, Paul was often in peril. He spent years writing letters of hope, not from a comfy chair snuggled up in front of a fire as I'm doing now, but from the floor of a prison cell. His message of hope was not for future Olympic athletes but for those who find themselves surrounded by prison walls of loneliness, despair, fatigue, sickness, death, and other difficulties.

Your child's talents and personality traits are, to some extent, built into his or her DNA, but that doesn't get you out of the job of parenting. What is not predetermined is his or her character. While it's not likely you'll make an Olympic athlete out of a child who has no natural ability, you can teach and train that not-so-athletic child to be kind to others, to respect others' property, to open doors for older women, to share what he or she has, and to be the kind of person who makes a positive impact on the world.

PART TWO

IDENTIFYING THE CHARACTER TRAITS YOU WANT TO SEE IN YOUR CHILDREN

PUTTING IT ALL TOGETHER

It's time to take a closer look at some of the character traits we, as parents, would like to develop in our children. This is not intended to be a complete list. You might think of other traits that you feel are valuable, but this list is a good beginning.

Honest
Compassionate
Loving
Kind
Patient
Joyful
Gentle
Self-controlled
Loyal
Reliable
Consistent
Persistent
Humble
Just
Encouraging
Merciful
Stable
Strong
Mature
Disciplined
Sincere
Trustworthy

In the *Pick Two* introduction I explained why I chose *strong* and *kind* as the two character traits I wanted to instill in our children. (By the way, I want them to have many other good traits as well; these two are simply where we started.) Let's delve a little deeper now into the two traits I chose and then look closer at some of the other valuable traits. I hope this will help you choose two character traits you most want to see in your children.

As you're reading, think about how you acquired each trait. Did someone help you? Did you learn it through life experiences? Did you read about it? How you acquired a certain trait is important in that we most often repeat what we have been taught. This happens all the time with more tangible traits. For instance, if your dad valued hard work, most likely you were taught to work hard. If your mom valued music, most likely you took piano or guitar lessons.

Look back over the list and put a check beside or circle the qualities you value and hope to see in your children. You will be tempted to check all of them, but when you select one trait, several more will automatically fall under it. Or you may want to wait and pick two after reading the next section. Either way, I believe that choosing two to focus on will help you to be very specific in your prayers and other actions as you strive to meet your goal.

1. Two-mama meeting the grandchildren at the flagpole to pray for another great school year, 2008. This woman does more than you will ever know (L to R: Bella, Aevin, Asa, Will, Aslyn).

2. Papaw Phil about to baptize John Luke, 2009. We are thankful to have such a strong spiritual legacy in our family. Passing it on!

3. Mamaw Jo surrounded by all her grandkids and great-grandkids at her annual Christmas brunch, 2014. This picture is full of love.

4. Miss Kay with Rebecca at Duck and Dressing, 2014. Miss Kay is always there with a hug, a kind word, and a biscuit to make your day better.

5. Two-papa with Sadie on the Duck Commander Cruise, 2014. The grandkids say he's the one who never says no. If anyone wants to go get a snow cone, ask Two-papa—he'll take you every time!

1. First day of kindergarten for Sadie and first grade for John Luke, 2002.
2. This back-to-school picture should win an award for funniest! It captures each kid's thoughts about the day perfectly, 2011.
3. Tell me how you feel about the first day of school, 2012!
4. Rebecca's LSU graduation, 2012.
5. They are growing up too fast! First day of school, 2013.
6. John Luke's last first-day-of-school picture, 2014. Love his choice of clothes!

1. Rebecca and John Luke on our family vacation in Disney World, the first year Rebecca joined our family, 2006.
2. Rebecca graduating from LSU, 2012. She's ready to take on the world!
3. Rebecca and her model, Sadie, at Senior Fashion Show, 2012. Rebecca designed and made the dress from recycled clothes that she found at Goodwill.
4. Rebecca with one of the sweet kids we get to love on in the Dominican Republic, 2014.
5. Rebecca at beach vacation, 2014. I am so proud of the woman she has become.

1. John Luke is one year old! Our first official family photo, 1996.
2. John Luke at two, 1997. I loved those blonde curls. I had a hard time cutting them!
3. John Luke hanging out with Willie at Camp Ch-Yo-Ca, 2000. He loved "working" with his dad.
4. A bunch of southern gentlemen (L to R): John Luke, Reeves Walker (family friend), and Cole and Reed Robertson (cousins), 2014.
5. Mary Kate's first trip to the Dominican Republic with John Luke, 2014. I'm sure there will be many more.

1. Sadie's first Easter, 1998. That smile!
2. Sadie and her dimples—soft smiles and flowers, 2002.
3. Can you tell Sadie loves *Survivor*?! Halloween, 2005: John Luke as Charlie Chaplin and Cole as a nerd.
4. Sadie's track medals from her freshman year, 2011. She's an athlete!
5. Sadie as Princess Peach. This is the costume fitting for the finale dance on *Dancing with the Stars*, 2014.

1. John Luke and Will. Brotherly love, 2002.
2. Will loved Buzz Lightyear. Halloween, 2003.
3. Loretta Lynn and Kenny Rogers, aka Bella and Will, performing at Grandparents Day at school, 2010.
4. Making the video for "Timber" with Matty B, 2012.
5. On the sidelines at a Saints game, 2013. Some father and son time.

1. Bella is ready to tackle her big brother Will. With the two of them only ten months apart, we had our hands full, 2002.
2. Bella posing for me at the beach, 2004. Such a cutie!
3. Bella showing off her Buck Commander hat, 2006. Life with her is never boring.
4. Bella all ready for her cheer competition, 2014. The family was there to cheer her on.
5. Opening night for the Duck Commander musical, 2015. Bella and her two moms—Ginna Claire Moffett, on the right, playing the role of me in the musical.

SEVEN

STRONG

The word *strength* is most often associated with our physical muscles. We all understand the concept of what it takes to be physically strong. But *strong* has other, deeper meanings. Two words associated with strength that I love are *resilience* and *sturdiness*.

RESILIENCE

Oh, how I hope my children will be resilient. One good definition of *resilience* is the ability to spring back into shape after being bent, stretched, or compressed.[1] Let's read that definition again. *The ability to spring back into shape after being bent, stretched, or compressed.* A good visual image of that is a rubber band. You can bend, wad up, stretch out, or wrap a rubber band around any shape, but when you let it go, it will always go back to its original shape. Wouldn't you love to be that way yourself, and wouldn't you love for your children to be like that? That would mean that when another child crushes their spirits by telling them they can't sing, they would bounce back and belt out a verse of Taylor Swift's hit song, "Shake It Off." That would mean that when a misguided teacher tells your child that math might not be his subject, he would put two and two together and say that math might not be, but something else *will* be. That means that when your child reaches adulthood and her husband walks out on their marriage, she grieves, but she doesn't forget her value and her worth. To be resilient is to truly understand that God will never leave you; that with Him, all things are possible; and no matter what challenges life throws at us, we are more than conquerors. We are overcomers!

STURDINESS

When I think of the word *sturdy*, I think about the four oak trees at the corners of my house when I was growing up. The branches of those oak trees have been through a lot. They've been covered in ice, tossed around by strong winds, struck by lightning, and climbed on by little kids, yet they still stand, providing shade and protection from the sun and the rain. I know our children will have days that will cause them to want to hide under the tree instead of being the tree. On those days I want them to be able to stay strong and be sturdy.

John Luke has a resilient and sturdy personality. When he was younger, he loved pets and had every pet possible. The only problem was that his pets didn't survive long. In a few short years we buried a cat, a dog, a rabbit, a horse, two goats, and several fish. Sadly, our little John Luke learned to live with this tragedy at a young age, but it never seemed to dampen his spirits or his love for adventure.

One day we were going to a restaurant to eat dinner with my mom. After we arrived, John Luke jumped out of the car and began climbing to the roof of our van. Since I was unbuckling and pulling from car seats three younger kids, I wasn't paying much attention to John Luke, who, at seven, I considered to be my "big kid." Like any good grandma, my mom saw him climbing and told him to get down. "Two-mama," he told her, "you have to see this!" And it was quite a sight to see. It seems a tiny frog had hitched a ride into town on our van, and our animal-loving John Luke had watched his journey from inside the van.

I've thought about that little frog over the years and how strong he had to be to make that trip into town. You see, it wasn't even his trip to make. He accidentally got on a fast-moving car headed to someplace he never dreamed he would go. But what a journey he had, and what a sweet surprise it was for a little boy to be a part of. That frog was strong and sturdy, and no matter what twists and turns came his way, he didn't let go. Even if the ride took paths he didn't plan to take, he held on strong until the ride was over.

My mom has likened our journey with *Duck Dynasty* to the journey that little frog took. She is often asked to speak at events, and she tells people that not one of the Robertsons set out to be a TV star. She's right. None of what has happened during the last few years of our lives is consistent with the lives we thought we would be living, but we are hanging on for the ride.

BIGGER THAN OUR DREAMS

While we've all had incredible journeys, the journey our Sadie took on *Dancing with the Stars* has truly amazed us. As we sat in the audience during that first show, we couldn't help but think of how shy Sadie was as a little girl. She was always making us laugh and entertaining us in the privacy of our own home, but out and about she would hardly even smile at the sweet ladies who talked to her at church. She was our child that I had to pry off of my arm to go to preschool. She cried every morning of her first year of school until Christmas break. I have a picture in my mind of her at the closing program of Camp Ch-Yo-Ca her first year as a day camper. She didn't want to stand in front of all the parents and sing at the program, but I made her go up there. She stood on the front row and cried the entire time. Never sang a note.

Even though Sadie was shy and had a hard time showing her fun little personality in front of people when she was young, we knew she had a light and the ability to use it, so we worked to never allow her to give in to her fears. Even through our tears, we encouraged her to get up there and do it. Watching Sadie go first on opening night of *Dancing with the Stars*, sitting on top of that giant birthday cake, we thought back to the days of *making* her speak up when adults spoke to her. She confidently whipped her ponytail and then took over the dance floor, and that's when you saw the waterworks from Willie. (You can find Sadie's first dance on the show on YouTube.) It was a proud moment for us as her mom and dad. This was not something that she would have ever thought she could do.

Fortunately for all of us, God's dreams for our lives are bigger than our dreams. Many years ago I heard a song titled "Shepherd Boy." In it the writers suggest that when others see a shepherd boy, God may see a king. The song references King David in the Bible, but you can see that God has great plans for all of our children. He sees leaders, encouragers, missionaries, preachers, and teachers.

God saw a future for Sadie that she could not see. Our job was to help her develop the skills she needed to answer whatever call God had for her life. Even though by the time Sadie was asked to be on *Dancing with the Stars* she had overcome her shyness, as she was contemplating accepting the offer, fear and doubt began to creep in. At one point when she was verbalizing her concerns, it was her little sister, Bella, who said to her, "Is this Sadie talking, or is this fear talking?" Those wise words helped Sadie realize she really did have the strength to take the journey God laid out before her and that God did not give us a spirit of fear. It's from His Spirit living in us that our true strength comes.

There will be times in life when our children will get on a ride that wasn't of their making. It will seem like the best thing to do is to abandon ship, but if we can teach our kids to hold on, to be sturdy through the storms of life, the outcome might be better than they ever imagined it could be.

Willie's Words on Being Strong

Someone once said being a parent isn't for wimps. I agree. I've had to be strong in ways I never dreamed possible. I guess now I'm thinking about changing those dirty diapers and cleaning up after the kids when they were sick. That's an inner strength I'm not sure I knew I had. But now the kids are past the dirty-diaper-and-throw-up stage, and I have to be strong in another way.

Wanting to be a strong parent and raise well-behaved children should be as natural as knowing that if the house was on fire, you would get them out. In that situation, with flames surrounding your children, there would be no thought about whether you would carry your children to safety. You would just do it.

Dangerous flames present themselves today in many other ways: the Internet, TV, bad friends, cell phones, bad movies, drugs. All of these things are just as dangerous to our children. We have to be strong enough to let them know we are their protectors. It's fascinating to me that children as young as two can sniff out the weaknesses in adults caring for them. They will test to see how far they can go and what they can get away with. They will depend on a strong parent to help them get through some tough growing-up years. Having a strong parent is the best chance for raising a strong child.

Growing up on the banks of a river in West Monroe, Louisiana, my brothers and I spent a lot of time together. There weren't as many distractions as children face today. We made up games, played hard, and fished and hunted together. At times we solved arguments by fighting, which I'm glad that my kids don't do much, but that's how it was at the time. Jase and I probably fought the most. We are two and a half years apart, which seemed to fuel the fire when our tempers flared. Being the younger of the two, I felt I had to bow up because I was a bit smaller. No one tormented me more than Jase—which happens often with siblings—and growing up in a house where we all shared one bedroom didn't help. We were certainly tough. You would think that all the punching, thumping, and pinching would be reasons for us being strong today—and you would be partially right. But I think my brothers and I are strong today because our parents left us alone to figure things out. We might not have always gotten it right, but we did it.

I want my children to have an inner strength that comes from working things out on their own and, if they can't work it out, knowing their parents are there to help them. I always knew my parents were there for me, but they let me think for myself and try before they interfered. My kids are all strong in different ways, and I know that's how all people are. I do what I can to encourage the areas they are strong in and build up the areas they aren't.

EIGHT

KIND

My sweet grandmother, Mamaw Howard, loved to quote Bible verses to her grandkids. She would write them out for us on those white sheets of paper that came in pantyhose packages. One of her favorites was Ephesians 4:32: "Be *kind* and compassionate to one another, forgiving each other, just as in Christ God forgave you." I can still hear her quoting that verse with great emphasis on the word *kind*. The first rule of teaching your children kindness is letting them see it in you. Children learn ethical values by watching the adults in their lives. Hearing my grandmother speak these words and watching her, as well as my other grandparents and my parents, treat others kindly is why I value this trait so much.

Willie and I want to teach our children that kindness should never be conditional, based on someone else's behavior. In other words, teach your children to be kind no matter what other people do. We never know how valuable a kind word might be to that person. But that should not be the reason for treating someone kindly. We should be kind because God has asked us to be that way.

GIVE YOUR KIDS OPPORTUNITIES TO SERVE

A great way to train your children to be kind is to help them expand the circle of people they care about. I have to give my grandmother credit for this one, too, as she loved to visit the folks at one of our local nursing homes. When I was growing up, she would go every week, taking home-made cookies to share with the residents and taking me or one of my cousins with her. We learned to be concerned for people with whom we weren't directly associated in any other way. We learned to seek out those less fortunate and to include them in our prayers.

My family has always been active in mission efforts. My siblings and I started going on mission trips as teenagers, and now our children go on at least one mission trip a year. Again, this broadens their outlook on life and makes them aware of the needs of others. Our children cannot know about the needs of others if we don't show them.

There are so many ways to expand your children's world. Find an organization, such as Help One Now, World Vision, or Compassion International, that will allow you and your children to sponsor a child in a Third World country. This is such a great way to show them how to be kind to those you may not know personally but of whose plight you've become aware. In our home there is always a picture on our refrigerator of a child we are sponsoring—a child we are giving to and praying for, even though we will probably never see him or her in this lifetime. It helps us see the world as much bigger than our own backyard.

SPREAD KINDNESS

There have been movements to spread kindness in our country. I'm sure you've heard of Random Acts of Kindness or the Campaign for Kindness. Even with these great efforts, there is so much unkindness in social media and on television. Read your teenager's Twitter or Instagram page, and you'll be shocked at how unkind teenagers can be to one another.

Kindness is defined as "the quality of being friendly, generous, and considerate."[1] Studies have shown that people who express gratitude and are helpful and generous to others are more likely to be happy and healthy. I am thrilled to know that as we strive to produce kind children, they're also likely to be happy children.

While it's true that children come in all shapes and sizes, they do not come to us as kind or unkind. They need the adults in their lives to help them become caring, considerate, thoughtful, and respectful of others. It's a challenge we all have to rise to as we strive to leave this world a better place than we found it.

Willie's Words on Being Kind

I must admit, all that testosterone in small quarters as I was growing up made being kind a little harder to accomplish. I'm pretty sure my brothers and I were all kinder to other people than we were to one another, but my mom tried. We were taught to be kind, and I think I was born with a kindness gene. I will never forget a fight that broke out between two eighth graders on a bus ride home from school when I was probably in the fourth grade. One boy smacked the other guy in the face with his brass knuckles and cut him pretty badly. It was probably over a girl, as most of these fights seemed to be, but I felt so bad for the guy. He was a new guy on our bus, and the guy who punched him was a total bully. I started bawling. All the older girls on the bus tried to comfort me, but I was crushed. I always made a special effort after that day to talk to the new kid who got punched. He probably didn't care since I was just a little fourth grader, but I tried to show him kindness after seeing that happen to him.

I also loved to help the less fortunate at school. It was a small country school, and there was always some little kid or person who got made fun of. I admit I was pretty popular. I was athletic, made good grades, and had some killer dimples. I seemed to have friends from all walks of life: jocks, pretty girls, and kids who were not popular by other fourth graders' standards, which were not that good. I remember talking to Mom about a kid in my class who was very poor. He smelled awful all the time, so naturally he was a target for bullies. I asked her what I could do to help him. We came up with a plan to put soap secretly in his backpack. I figured there simply wasn't any at his house. In no way did I mean it as a joke. I just wanted to be kind to him and save him from the bullies and help him smell a bit better. I like to think I helped him.

We make it a point to show our kids the importance of being kind to others. One day I noticed that Sadie had left a note and a piece of candy as a thank-you to the lady who helps clean our house. I was a proud dad at that moment. I knew that Sadie was learning the value of kindness. My other children have done acts of kindness like this, too, and I'm always proud when I see this. I know they have to see kindness in me first so I work at it too. I don't think you can ever be too kind. Just can't happen.

NINE

SELF-CONTROLLED

Self-control—or actually the lack thereof—gets many of us in trouble. Self-control is "the ability to control oneself, in particular one's emotions and desires or the expression of them in one's behavior, especially in difficult situations."[1] Essentially, self-control is learning to keep both our behavior and our emotions in check.

When I hear the word *self-control*, I first think of a diet. I recognize that's an American response, as we're one of the few countries where we have the luxury of overeating—and we do that very well. But self-control is more than being able to push away the ice cream; it's learning to set appropriate boundaries in every area of life: relationships, eating, drinking, volunteering, shopping, and expressing our emotions.

THE BLESSINGS OF BOUNDARIES

Boundaries are designed to control something. We start establishing boundaries for our children as soon as they can roll over. We put a pillow or some other object on the bed so they can't roll off. As they get older, we fence in the yard or place a safety barrier in front of the stairs. Our purpose is to control them for their own protection because they are not yet capable of protecting themselves.

As our children grow even older, our boundaries become rules: "No playing ball in the road," or "Curfew is at eleven o'clock." We establish these boundaries to protect our children and teach them self-control.

It's important to help them see that boundaries or rules, when followed, make life easier.

Think about it: if you tell your kids that you're going to play a new card game with them, one of them is sure to ask, "What are the rules?" As much as everyone complains about having to follow rules, it's the first thing people want to know before the first card is played. That's because we have an innate understanding that rules actually make games more fun. It's never fun when no one knows or understands the rules. It's chaotic and crazy. If kids can learn this principle, they will be happier little people. They'll understand that rules do the same thing for life as they do for a game, keeping things orderly and fair so everyone has more fun.

As I've already mentioned, our family is connected to a summer camp for kids. One year my mom was in charge of the camp's nighttime activity. She decided it would be fun to play a basketball game with no rules. As you can imagine, it wasn't fun at all. Kids were getting hurt and mad, and the adults were running around trying to gain some control. Afterward, it inspired a great time of reflection as the staff and campers discussed how it related to our lives. We safeguard against having a life that is like one big, crazy, out-of-control basketball game by following the boundaries God set for us.

Having self-control means that you can enforce the rules yourself. An adult dieter might tell himself that he cannot eat bread for a month. It's his own rule; no one is going to enforce it. No diet police will be patrolling his kitchen; the dieter has to do it alone. More important issues include controlling your temper, making good choices in relationships, limiting time spent with technology, and balancing work and relaxation. Every area of our life is affected by our ability to control ourselves or set personal boundaries.

If you have ever read about the now-famous marshmallow experiment, you know that this was a study to see if children were willing to wait (use delayed gratification) for the treat of two marshmallows instead of the one they were offered at first. The experiment made for some funny scenes of children either gobbling up the one marshmallow as soon as the researcher left the room or squirming and trying to entertain themselves to keep their minds off the marshmallow sitting on the table. The most interesting part of this study came years later as the researchers followed up on those children. They found that the children who had been willing to wait scored higher on the SAT, had lower levels of substance abuse, responded better to stress, and exhibited other great traits we want our children to have. Basically, the study showed that we need to learn that good things come to those who are willing to wait and that most successful endeavors require us to forgo the easy and do something a little bit harder.[2]

THE CHOICE TO OBEY

Think back to Adam and Eve in the garden of Eden. God told them they were free to eat anything, with one exception. Think of it: God had given them an endless supply of the finest fruits, berries, and nuts. There was no cooking. *It was Paradise!* And they could have all of it if they would obey just one rule. So here was God's test, and as we know, they didn't pass. Satan tempted Eve until she could no longer control herself, and she ate from the forbidden tree. God set a boundary and watched as first Eve and then Adam crossed it. (It might be significant that their failure involved food. Self-control around food has been difficult from the beginning!)

God *knows* that His children have free will. God *wants* His children to have free will. That's how He created us. You want your children to have free will too. I know, sometimes it would be nice if they didn't, but who wants a robot child? It was important to God for His children to obey Him by their own choice.

We also know, from the rest of the story, that God didn't stop loving His disobedient children; rather, He loved them so much that He continued to try to guide them down the right path. Had Adam and Eve been able to resist the temptations of the devil and look only to God, their lives—and in fact, our lives—would have been remarkably different. The same is true for our children. If we can teach our children to obey and respect the rules of our household and the community they live in, great blessings will await them. When they don't, we won't give up on them; we'll continue to love them and guide them down the right path.

Willie's Words on Being Self-Controlled

I was a youth minister for several years after college before coming back to work for Duck Commander. During my time in youth ministry, I saw so many kids who did not have self-control. This made me really want to see this trait in my own kids. As I watched kids make poor decisions, I knew they were doing things they would regret later. Many times an action they did affected them the rest of their lives. Of course, some of the poor decisions teens make are not because of poor parenting; they are just because teens aren't always wise. But I did see many situations where parents could have stepped in when the teen was younger and possibly helped that child gain some self-control.

I've never been a fan of kids who are totally out of control. Not only is it annoying to be around, it's often a sign of trouble to come as the children grow older. It seems that babies are born pretty calm, but it doesn't take long for them to get their own personalities and get out of control. We've all seen kids who throw a fit and don't care whether they are in public or private. Basically they are saying, "I do not want to be controlled by anything or anybody." It's pretty sad and embarrassing to see out-of-control behavior in a kid, but it's really bad to see it in an adult, maybe even a parent. I've seen parents who lose control in heavy traffic or at their children's ball games, and I have to wonder if they don't see this lack of self-control in themselves.

These same parents seem surprised when their own kids cannot control themselves. It's a pretty bad scene to witness: lots of screaming, then crying, and nobody is in control.

Having self-control involves many different stages of development. It is another one of those areas that has to start when children are young. When John Luke was young, he could throw some great fits—I mean, I'm-going-to-make-life-miserable-for-everyone fits. When we would go to grab him, he would arch his back in such a way that it was hard to hold him. I knew he was fighting for control. In his fight for control he became out of control, as people often do. He wanted someone to notice how out-of-control he was as he tried to gain control of some situation he wasn't happy about.

Whenever John Luke started blowing a gasket about something, I would take him and hold him. As John Luke would twist and contort himself like a little human pretzel, I applied what I like to call "the daddy straitjacket." I wrapped my arms around his arms and held him tightly. The more he fought, the less I would let him move. This was a simple way to let him know that he was not in control and that we, his parents, were not going to let him throw a fit just because he didn't get his way. The whole process only took about five minutes before he wore himself out. Usually he would fall fast asleep. Both of my boys seemed to struggle more with keeping themselves under control than my girls. Hmm. I'm not really surprised by this.

In today's world we've seen enough fit-throwers on TMZ. We sure don't want to see our children on there, and we don't want to be on there either. Even as adults, we have to continually work to stay in control. I'll admit that Korie and I struggled our first year of marriage. I would fly off the handle for the simplest things. But we determined to get better, and we did. Self-control is not so hard that we can't do it. We can all have self-control.

When I was growing up, Phil and Kay were big on letting us boys sort of govern ourselves. There weren't a whole lot of rules, and Dad never yelled or screamed. He was always in control and always calm. We knew he had a different side from his past. We knew that at one point he had little self-control, but we never saw that side. We didn't *want* to see that side. I think knowing this was part of what kept Jase and me on the straight path. Al and Jep wandered off the path for a time but got back on the right path pretty quickly.

Remember, we can do all the right things with our kids, and they still might struggle with self-control. The answer to the problem of no self-control is the same as the answer for everything else—faith in God. Phil and Kay instilled a faith in us and relied on that to teach us self-control. When we yield control to God, then we will have the self-control we need to make it in this life.

TEN

HONEST

Have you ever talked to someone who has a habit of saying "honestly" before practically every sentence? Was everything he or she said prior to that comment dishonest? I don't think so. It's just a silly habit. Someone who is honest is good and truthful and does not hide the truth. But, honestly, honesty comes with a lot of gray areas. Perhaps it's one of the grayest of the character traits, which makes teaching our children to be honest a challenge. Every day our children will encounter varying levels of honesty and will need to know how to navigate the honesty waters with a strong paddle. Your example will be extremely important, as children become aware of the difference between truth and falsehood at a young age.

HONESTY WITH DISCRETION

Honesty is a trait we must teach in our homes, but honesty involves discretion. Choosing to be honest never means choosing to hurt someone else for the sake of honesty. My younger brother, Ryan, was an honest child. He basically said everything that came to his mind. When he was young, it was cute and funny. When he was four and told a woman at church, "You know, if you went on a diet, you could lose some weight," it wasn't the best thing to say to someone, but he was four! As he got older, I remember my mom saying more than once, "Ryan, you don't have to say everything you think." She had to teach him to value holding his tongue out of kindness to others as much as she did honesty. My mom often used to say to all of us—but especially to him—"If you can't say something nice, don't say anything at all."

As adults, we understand that sometimes you have to say things that aren't nice. You have to deal with difficult things in life. But for our children, I think this is a good principle to teach when relating to others. Think about what you are about to say, and if it doesn't come from a place of kindness and respect for their feelings, then just keep it to yourself.

Isn't it funny how kids and old people can get away with saying pretty much anything they want? Sadie was my most honest child in that regard. She would ask my grandmother about her wrinkles or my mom about the veins on her hands. One time I remember holding my breath for a minute, worried about what was going to come out of her mouth. She was probably four or five years old, and we were at the house of a friend whose babysitter had a couple of gold teeth. I could tell that Sadie was staring at her. Sadie suddenly asked, "How'd you get those gold teeth?" As it turned out, Sadie thought they were fabulous and seriously wanted to know where she could get some, so all turned out well. The woman told her she had gotten them at the dentist's office, and Sadie ran off to play. Whew!

Some would argue that teaching children to be discreet teaches them to be dishonest, but I would argue against that. One definition of *honest* is "honorable in principles, intentions, and actions; upright and fair."[1] Synonyms include *authentic, decent, sincere, true,* and *trustworthy.* These are all positive, good traits that we want our children to have; these words don't fit a person who just blurts out whatever is on her mind. The definition of *dishonest* is "characterized by lack of truth, honesty, or trustworthiness: unfair, deceptive."[2] Synonyms for *dishonest* include *fraudulent, corrupt, deceptive, shady,* and *underhanded*—all traits that we certainly don't want our children to have.[3]

Don't Excuse Lying

Now for the other side of the coin. While some kids, like my brother, are born with an honest gene, others seem to be born with, to put it politely, an aversion to telling the truth. While all children lie at one time or another and must be taught that lying is wrong, some definitely seem to have a harder time learning this lesson. I won't mention any names, ahem, but we do have a child like that. Now, I will say that he's not very good at it; he gives a lot of telltale signs. He looks away, his voice gets a little tighter and higher—but he tries, oh, he tries.

When children are young, we sometimes excuse their lying because we think it's funny or cute and they're just kids. But do not take lying lightly. Just as being overly honest can be cute when you're four but rude when you're twenty-four, lying can't help but be destructive and danger-ous to your children and to their relationships. The Bible calls lying a sin (see Prov. 12:22), and we must treat it as such from a young age so that our children understand the severity of it in our lives.

The Robertsons love to tell stories. We all joke that some stories grow every time they're told. Si even admits that his stories are 95 percent truth-ful. I'm thinking even that might be overstating things! This is meant all in good fun, though. However, I have a nephew who, when he was young, didn't just embellish stories; he totally made them up. What was funny at first soon became something for his parents to deal with. They wanted their child to be a truthful adult, so they had some work to do to make sure he understood the difference between a lie and the truth.

Here's an example from our creative little nephew. One day when we were at the beach, John Luke said that he'd seen a jellyfish in the ocean. John Luke's cousin, who shall remain nameless, quickly countered, "I saw a shark last night."

We said, "Come on, now, we were with you yesterday at the beach, and we didn't see a shark. How did you see one?"

He said, "I got up at four o'clock in the morning and went down to the beach and saw a shark. I promise; I did." He was five at the time. We all knew he was lying, and by the end, I think he knew that we knew he was lying, but he never gave up the story that he woke up in the middle of the night, walked down to the beach, and saw a shark.

How to Deal with a Child Who Lies

How do you deal with children and lying? This can be a tough one because sometimes it's difficult to prove that someone is lying. But when you do catch a child not telling the truth, deal with it with an appropriate punishment. When I caught our kids doing something they weren't supposed to do, I would often say, "Before I ask you this question, I'm going to tell you that if you lie about this, your punishment will be much worse. Before you answer, take a breath and think hard about what you're going to say, and make sure it's the truth." If our kids told the truth, even if what they had done was wrong, we would just talk to them about why it was wrong without punishing them. However, if they lied about it, punishment was guaranteed.

As children grow older, that warning might not be necessary or warranted because they should know better than to lie about whatever they did. But when they're young, it teaches them that they should take every opportunity to tell the truth. If they think they might be in trouble, the first instinct for some children is to lie, even if they haven't done anything wrong after all. In those cases, reminding them to tell the truth from the very beginning can help them learn to do the right thing.

Children have the ability to watch and learn, but teaching them good character traits like honesty requires intentionality. When your children are two and a half or three, test them in this area. Ask, "How many eyes do you have?" They should be able to answer appropriately. Then say, "I have three." This should bother them; so then say, "I don't have three, do I? I have only two, just like you." Explain to your children that you were not telling the truth so that you could teach them what telling the truth means. Explain how very important honesty is to your family. This is one simple way to start the conversation, which is important because what typically happens is that we wait for our children to display dishonesty before we start a conversation about being honest.

Your child will try dishonesty. It's inevitable. Your child will be confronted about something, and he or she will try to avoid negative consequences by not telling the truth.

Lying starts as a way to avoid consequences. But once a child receives positive feedback from lying, it could become a bad habit because lying can bring what the child considers to be positive results. Bragging or exaggerating can make him or her feel more accepted. Lying can also be a form of laziness. Some people think it's easier to lie because telling the truth usually requires some action or change. My grandpa used to say, "That fella lies when the truth would make a better story." Some people lie so often, they don't know that the truth is better.

The Importance of Being Honest

I cannot overstate the importance of being honest. Although it may seem at times that being dishonest will help us get ahead, in truth, that's a lie. Honesty can take a person further in life than many other great traits. Honest people are respected and can be trusted because they stand on their word, and their word is truth.

My dad and my grandfather started many businesses in our community, and to this day, one of the greatest compliments I hear about them is how honest they were in their business dealings. When we encounter an honest person, it can restore our faith in mankind. Dealing with honest people is such a refreshing and positive experience. One's reputation in life is more important than any physical gain. We must train our children to be honest and teach them that dishonesty brings painful consequences. Being honest might make us uncomfortable for a few minutes, but it leads to much greater rewards.

Willie's Words on Being Honest

There's not much I hate worse than to see my kids be dishonest. However, there's a time in almost all kids' lives when they don't want to be punished for something they did wrong, or they don't want to do their homework or clean up the mess they made, and they simply don't tell the truth.

Whatever the reason, we work to stop this as soon as possible in our home because we know the destructive path it can lead to. If we allow our children to lie and get away with it when they are young, they will do that in their marriages, their friendships, or at their jobs as an adult. If you aren't honest about the small things, how can others trust you to be honest about the big things?

One tip in helping your kids stay honest, however, is do not back your kids into a corner so they think they must lie to avoid repercussions. We make sure to let them know that honesty is always the best answer even if it's 'fessing up to something big and bad that they did wrong. I want our kids to feel free to tell the truth and to know that the truth is always the best answer.

ELEVEN

COMPASSIONATE

When our children reach double digits, we begin taking them to the Dominican Republic to help with a children's home we support there, do work with the local church, and offer medical care to the sick of the community. We want our children, at a young age, to be exposed to a world totally different from the safe, comfortable world they live in. They see children who don't get enough to eat. They see houses that barely protect the people inside from rain and heat. They see sickness with no possibility of a cure.

Compassion is the emotional response we feel when we are exposed to the needs of others. According to one definition, *compassion* is "a deep awareness of and sympathy for another's suffering."[1] Our God is such a compassionate God. All through the Bible, stories of God's compassion should bring us to our knees, touching our hearts so that we want to show love to those who are less fortunate than we are. In the Old Testament God is described again and again as a God of compassion. Psalm 86:15 says, "You, Lord, are a compassionate and gracious God, / slow to anger, abounding in love and faithfulness." And Psalm 145:9 says, "The LORD is good to all; / he has compassion on all he has made."

Compassion is more than feeling sorry for someone; it's acting on those feelings. I'm so grateful that our church family is involved in mission work both within the United States and abroad. As parents, we often want to shield our children from seeing such need, but please don't. They need to be exposed to the plight of others so that they will be moved to do something to help. Compassion for others is a gift we give ourselves. There is no greater joy than bringing hope to those without hope.

Each summer when we visit the Dominican Republic, we spend time with the children playing games, doing crafts, and singing; but we also evaluate their needs. A few summers ago we noticed that one precious little girl had a bed that was sinking in the middle. In fact, the middle nearly touched the ground. After some haggling with the local store owner, we were the proud owners of a new bed for Maria. None of us will ever forget Maria's face when she looked in her room and saw a new bed. We all cried tears of joy!

WE NEED EACH OTHER

Developing compassion helps children understand that we need each other; we are part of a larger community that needs and depends on others for survival. The old saying "No man is an island" is true. Ecclesiastes 4:12 tells us that one might be overpowered, and two have a better chance, but "a cord of three strands is not quickly broken."

I know some personalities enjoy being alone more than others. John Luke and Rebecca function well when alone, but Sadie, Will, and Bella would rather take a sibling or a friend along than go somewhere by themselves. Our God-given personalities factor into all that we do, but God designed us for companionship. He made man and said that it wasn't good for him to be alone. God didn't say, "Man cannot cook or clean or remember it's his mother's birthday, and man can't possibly raise a child . . ." It's not that man *couldn't* do any of those things alone; God said that it wasn't good. Man needs a companion. Without others there's little need to have any of the character traits we are discussing in this book. Why be kind if there is no one to be kind to?

COMPASSION BEGINS AT HOME

As I've said before, we learn to function first in our immediate families. This is where our character traits are first challenged. Think about the older sibling who has already been through the pain of new braces. That sibling can be either compassionate and sympathetic toward the younger sibling or uncaring, rude, and unkind. Hateful, unkind people will struggle all through life because they will never connect with others. Compassionate people, however, will go through life understanding that they need others and others need them. That basic desire to be needed brings joy, happiness, and security. We all want to be happy and feel connected to others. Compassion is the emotion that takes a thought (*that child is starving*) and connects it to an action (*I will help in this way*). That action connects two or more people in a special way.

If you and your children have not participated in a compassion project, I strongly urge you to find one. You don't have to go out of the country; there are plenty of opportunities in your own town. Our church family supports a project to feed the hungry. On Wednesday nights church members place food in bags, and on Fridays, people are welcome to come and get what they need. This is another great example of showing compassion. Many of our children and teens come to the church building on Wednesday nights ready to pack bags; then, on Friday nights, they line up to help distribute the bags. Your local food bank is a good place to start if you don't know how to begin a ministry such as this one. But there are many more options.

If you want to be compassionate and want your children to be also, just ask God to open the doors of opportunity for you to show compassion. He will be happy to do that for you. Compassion cannot be lazy. Compassion requires action. A person who just looks at the situation and feels sadness is showing sympathy, but a person who actually does something to remedy or improve the situation is showing compassion. That's our goal: to raise children who not only see needs but feel compelled to act on them. That's how we change the world!

Willie's Words on Being Compassionate

This is one trait I think all parents really hope their children have. Actions certainly speak louder than words when it comes to compassion because having compassion is an action. Our faith teaches us that we must show compassion toward others, and examples like Jesus' showing compassion to a woman at a well show us how compassion works (John 4). That's the kind of compassion I want my children to have. Compassion does not just feel sorry for someone; it actually does something about the situation and makes a difference. Jesus' compassion for humanity ultimately caused Him to lay down His life for us.

I saw compassion in action in many ways when I was growing up. I saw my mom and dad take in many a rough character, feed them, and let them stay at our place, and my dad studied the Bible with them. We fed more people in our house than you can count. Seeing this helped me to understand and embrace what being compassionate really means.

Here's another great example of compassion. Growing up, we always wanted brand-name stuff, but Mom said we couldn't afford it. Dad had a buddy he played college football with he called "Hog." Hog had been successful in the oil business, and he would visit us from time to time. I think he came to hunt, but he loved to eat my mom's cooking too. (Apparently he'd been given that nickname for a reason.) Hog had two or three sons, and on one visit, he brought a box of clothes that his kids had outgrown, and they were *all* Polo brand clothes! You have never seen boys go so crazy. We didn't even care that some didn't fit. We were going to wear them anyway. I was so grateful, and I have never forgotten that one man's compassion on a bunch of redneck boys growing up on the river.

Korie has been instrumental in taking our kids to the Dominican Republic, where they get to help kids who are truly in need. They have learned to act on their compassion, just like Jesus did. John Luke and Sadie have also gone to other countries to help build houses, support schools, love on orphans, and encourage the local workers who work in those areas. It makes me happy that our kids, who grew up with more than I did, still understand the meaning of compassion.

One year I was invited by Chairman of the Joint Chiefs of Staff Martin Dempsey to go on the Christmas USO tour to Afghanistan. I said yes without hesitation, but later I was a little nervous about being in a war zone. Also, since it was the holiday season, my schedule was pretty crazy. But when I thought of what these men and women go through by being away from their children, spouses, parents, brothers, sisters, and loved ones, I was filled with compassion and wanted to do my part. I wasn't giving money or gifts, but I gave my time and energy. It was a great experience. The soldiers were so excited to see someone from the States. The general and I sang a song from *Duck the Halls: A Robertson Family Christmas*. The song was called "Hairy Christmas," so it was pretty funny. Everyone loved it and had a great time. I think they were mostly surprised the general could really sing.

Compassion should make you move. It should push you to help others and be there for them. I will never forget my trip to Afghanistan. Not everyone can do something like the USO tour, but all of us can do *something*. Show your children what compassion looks like. Whether it's feeding the poor, going on a mission trip, or just giving a hug to someone who is lonely, or even smelly, teach your children that nothing done in love is small. Small acts of kindness make a big difference.

I want my kids to know that compassion is not always about giving money. Sometimes giving money to people isn't the right thing to do. Sometimes it's holding someone's hand or hugging someone's neck. Teach your children to look around and see the need, then act on it.

TWELVE

PATIENT

B e patient!" If you are a parent, you've said this more than once because rare is the person who is born patient. We want what we want, and we want it now.

THE CONNECTION BETWEEN PATIENCE AND SUFFERING

So what is patience? A combination of definitions that I found during my research is this: *patience* is doing something in a careful way over a long period of time without hurrying.

After studying many definitions, my brain was still hungry for a little more information, so l looked up the root word of *patient* and found that it is the Latin word *patiens,* which is the present participle of *pati,* meaning "to suffer."[1] Finding that little bit of Latin trivia helped it all make sense to me. Now I understand why sick people are called patients—and why it so often feels like suffering when we have to wait.

Teaching some of our busy little ones to be patient is another reminder of the connection between patience and suffering. It can be as difficult as trying to stuff a square peg into a round hole. Some kids just seem wired to move quickly, and their skill set does *not* include patience or calmness.

We know that our personality or temperament affects how we approach every aspect of our lives, but having a certain personality type

75

doesn't change what God calls us to be. Romans 12:12 tells us to "be joyful in hope, patient in affliction, faithful in prayer." Moms, some of us have children who are not calm or patient by nature. These kids seem to have one foot out the door at all times, and for them being patient practically requires a ball and chain to hold them back.

Patience Is Life-Changing

Being patient is a skill that can be practiced and, while probably not completely mastered, improved upon. It's a life-changing skill! I put an exclamation point at the end of that sentence so you would really take it to heart. *Life-changing!*

Patience can lead to blessings beyond our wildest dreams, while a lack of patience can cause us to miss a blessing designed for us. God rewards those who successfully *wait* on Him, and to those who do not, He gives more time to practice their patience skills. We are given many examples in the Bible of this being true.

Remember the plight of Abraham in the Bible? God promised Abraham that his descendants would be as numerous as the sands on the seashore. Abraham was beginning to doubt God's fulfillment of this promise, as he and his wife, Sarah, were well past childbearing age and no baby was in sight. So Abraham took matters into his own hands and slept with his servant, Hagar, in order to have a baby with her and "help" God out. The full account of Abraham's lack of patience can be found in Genesis 16. Little did he know that God had a better plan. When Abraham was one hundred years old and Sarah was ninety years old, their son, Isaac, was born. It is through Isaac's line that our Savior, Jesus, was born.

Then there was Jacob, who labored for seven years to win his bride, Rachel. Genesis 29:20 says, "Jacob served seven years to get Rachel, but they seemed like only a few days to him because of his love for her." What a beautiful example of patiently waiting for a promised reward. Then we have the example in the New Testament of the son who decided he was tired of waiting for his inheritance and asked his father to give it to him early. He wasted his inheritance and woke up in a pigsty with no money left to live on.

In today's world we'd describe the foolish son in Luke 15 as being unable to delay gratification. The ability to delay gratification is patience. We live in a "microwave" world. Given the fast-paced nature of life today, patience may seem like the most outdated of all of the character traits. We put our food in a microwave oven, and if it's not warm in thirty seconds, we're irritated. In fact, waiting for popcorn for two and a half minutes is asking too much of us. We drive through a restaurant and expect warm food in our hands before one song is finished on the radio. If there's a delay and we're asked to pull off to the side and wait for three minutes, we do so but not without complaint. We turn on our computers and, if the website isn't up in less than five seconds, we complain that we have the slowest Internet carrier in the whole world. Some of these examples might be exaggerated, but we truly are an impatient society.

How great it is that our God is patient—even allowing us to have second chances. He waits patiently while we first try following our own path. Never turning His back on us, He holds us in His hands until we return to Him. I'm so grateful that He looks more closely at my heart than at my actions and patiently waits for my actions to be more reflective of my heart. Our God knows the value of patience, and if we truly love our children, we will do all that we can do to help them develop this character trait.

PATIENCE AND CONTENTMENT

An important aspect of patience is contentment. To be patient you must be content in the circumstance you find yourself in while you wait. The definition of *content* is to be in a state of peaceful happiness, satisfied. Can you say that you are satisfied? One of the problems in our society today is that we are never satisfied. We're always looking for something bigger, better, and faster. This has caused a culture in which young people jump from school to school, job to job, and move from town to town, never sticking with anything long enough to actually see the fruits of their success. I've often said that one key to the Robertson family's success in business and in life comes from being content.

The first year of Duck Commander, the business brought in only twelve thousand dollars. Not nearly enough to support a family of four growing boys and Granny and Pa, who lived with Phil and Miss Kay at the time. The second year wasn't much better. As a matter of fact, the first year *Duckmen of Louisiana* (the Duck Commander hunting DVD) was made, which was about ten years after Duck Commander started, only 600 copies were sold. Most people would have closed up shop and gone back to school teaching and coaching, but the Robertson family was patient. They gave the business time to grow, and during that time, they were content with what they had. They counted on commercial fishing to supplement their income. They ate what they caught in the river and what they killed and grew on their land. In their minds they had plenty. Willie says even though they qualified for free lunch at school because of their income, he never thought of his family as poor. They rarely bought new things, but they always had enough to eat, and there was plenty of happiness and joy in their home. There were many times when they could have given up and quit. Had they not been patient and content, Duck Commander never would have made it past the first few tough years. And millions of Americans would not have celebrated our fortieth anniversary with us on *Duck Dynasty*.

Willie's Words on Being Patient

Being kind was tough in a house full of boys, but being patient was even harder. Just sitting down at the dinner table was a test of patience. We all wanted the best piece of chicken or the biggest potato. After Dad said the prayer, it was game on, and we started reaching for the food. But there were ways we learned this important trait, and one of them was just by living in the outdoors and hunting and fishing.

I'm not the most patient guy and, I admit, I had to work at waiting for the fish to bite or the deer to come by my stand, but I finally figured it out. I don't know if there's a better way to learn that good things come to those who wait than being on the other end of a fishing pole or in a deer stand. Patience is all about learning to wait, and hunting and fishing are waiting sports.

I'm not a psychologist, but I think kids are born with different levels of patience. My brother Jase was born being able to sit still and wait for the fish to bite. John Luke is like Jase. He's naturally patient. Sadie is more like me. But whatever way we're born, we still have to learn that having patience is important.

The Bible says in 1 Corinthians 13:4 that "love is patient." That makes me think that when Korie or the kids are doing something that causes me to be late or miss something I want to do, my being patient and waiting on them shows them that I love them. Being patient is totally for the other person. I guess you can be patient with yourself, too, but mostly it's for someone else. Anytime we focus on someone else and not on ourselves, we are showing the kind of selfless love that God asks of us.

THIRTEEN

JOYFUL

You might be wondering why I use the word *joyful* instead of *happy, happy, happy*—especially since my father-in-law, Phil Robertson, has made that expression quite famous. At first glance *joyful* and *happy* seem like two words for the same emotion. It's true that the definitions are so similar, you might think you're dealing with just one word. *Happy* is defined as "feeling pleasure and enjoyment because of your life, situation, etc."[1] *Joy* is defined as "the emotion evoked by well-being, success, or good fortune, or by the prospect of possessing what one desires."[2] Yep, they sound just alike.

It's not until you look at the root word that you begin to see the difference. It has been said that experts in language and root meanings assert that translations used in the Bible for the word *joy* fall short of the original meaning. A more accurate word might be *gladness*, adding the concept of being appreciative.[3] That was a game changer for me. That tells me that being joyful is not simply being happy because circumstances are pleasant or fun; it's about being deeply grateful for those circumstances and for what transpired to cause the event.

Actually, being joyful is not even based on being happy. If I say that I'm happy today because I had a good day at work and then went out to eat with friends, I'm saying that conditions were right for me to have a happy feeling. But if I've had a rough day at work and gotten a flat tire on my way home but I'm still joyful, people who don't know me might think I've lost my mind. How can someone be joyful after a day like that?

Here's the answer: I could be joyful after a day like that because, unlike happiness, joy comes from a deeper place.

It's interesting to note that studies have been done to prove that, like other personality traits, happiness is somewhat determined by your genes. Any mom with more than one child will say that a study to prove that point was a waste of money—just spend a week with a group of children and be observant.

No doubt, genetics plays a part in whether you have a happy disposition. Some kids are just born happy. They wake up with a smile on their face. I met a little girl like this on my recent trip to Ethiopia. Her name is Martha, and I haven't stopped thinking about her smiling face since meeting her. She is two years old and has lived in an orphanage most of her life. The caregivers at the home didn't really know her story, only that she came to them at about six months old with some scars on her little body. She has had a difficult life, but this didn't stop Martha from smiling from ear to ear. Each day when we went to visit the orphanage, she was front and center on the front steps waving joyfully as our van pulled up the dirt road. There is no explanation for why Martha is joyful other than God built joy into her DNA.

Psychologists who study happiness believe that we can pursue happiness by doing away with negative emotions, such as pessimism and resentment, and concentrating on positive emotions, such as gratitude and love. I believe that we can train ourselves to act differently, and while it may be more difficult, we can train ourselves to think differently too. It's like the little boy who had been told repeatedly to sit down. The boy really did not want to sit down, but he realized he would face serious consequences if he didn't obey. He grudgingly sat down, but he looked at his mom and said defiantly, "I'm sitting down on the outside, but on the inside I'm standing up." I've gotten this look from my kids from time to time. You see, our actions don't always reflect our inner feelings, but in some cases it's still the right thing to do. In the end the child eventually forgets why he was mad in the first place and begins playing with whatever is around him.

A ROLE MODEL OF JOY

This subject cannot be addressed without our looking at one of the most joyful spiritual leaders in the Bible, Paul. Through Paul's eyes, we get to see that we can have a joyful spirit even when times are tough.

Paul was on fire for God after his conversion on the road to Damascus (Acts 9). Because of his preaching and teaching about Jesus, Paul found himself in prison on more than one occasion. Remarkably, he used his time in prison to encourage people who, while not in a physical prison, were in prisons of their own making: the prisons of self-doubt, worry, fear, anxiety, and sinful behavior. Paul made it very clear that his circumstances would not dictate his emotions. His joy, his peace, and his contentment were all rooted in something that went far deeper than the circumstances in which he found himself at the time of most of his writings.

Philippians is a book in the Bible devoted not to Paul's plight but to the plight of believers out in the world. Paul's words were written to encourage them. It becomes clear to the reader that Paul's joy came from a different place than most people's happiness. His joy came from a deep understanding of his mission and knowing that his mission was being completed even when his circumstances were not pleasant. Such an attitude could only come from a deep conviction that what he believed and preached to others was true.

Paul was sold on the gospel of Jesus Christ, so his perspective was not just from seeing the world through rose-tinted glasses. Instead, Paul was seeing the bigger picture. That's the only way a man could write and truly mean, "For Christ's sake, I delight in weaknesses, in insults, in hardships, in persecutions, in difficulties. For when I am weak, then I am strong" (2 Cor. 12:10). It's the reason he could encourage others with these words: "Do not be anxious about anything, but in every situation, by prayer and petition, with thanksgiving, present your requests to God" (Phil. 4:6). And it's the reason he could give these strong instructions to the believers at Philippi: "Rejoice in the Lord always. I will say it again: Rejoice!" (Phil. 4:4).

As superhuman as Paul may appear, everyone can do what he did. God didn't give Paul anything that we can't have, too, and Paul knew it. Many hold on to the encouragement in Philippians 4:13, and for good reason. It says, "I can do all this through him who gives me strength." Paul is saying that, in the face of difficult circumstances, even when we can't rejoice or be joyful in our own strength, we can rejoice through the power of Jesus Christ.

ANOTHER EXAMPLE OF JOY

Have you read the book or seen the movie *Unbroken*? It's the remarkable story of another man who spent many years in prison. That man was Louie Zamperini. While Louie's story is quite different from Paul's, their stories are remarkably similar. Paul was imprisoned because he was fighting for and defending Jesus Christ. Louie was imprisoned because he was defending and fighting for his country.

After Louie was released from his physical imprisonment, where he had endured brutal beatings, starvation, bitter cold, sickness, and more than I can relate to you, he became imprisoned in an even more profound way. He turned to alcohol to drown the nightmares that robbed him of sleep. He spent his days plotting revenge on his captors. He experienced outbursts of rage and nearly lost his wife and child because despair had overtaken him and he could see no way out. Louie told of meeting Jesus at a Billy Graham tent revival and immediately turning his life around. Only when he met the Lord and submitted his life to Him was he able to break out of the prison he had built around himself.

As I said, Louie and the apostle Paul had much in common. If you haven't read the account of Paul's conversion, take a look at it in Acts 9. Paul had been an angry man who persecuted Christians. His conversion was as immediate and complete as Louie Zamperini's was, and from the point of their conversion onward, both men spent their lives doing good for others. After giving his life to Jesus, Louie gave up his addiction to alcohol and never experienced another nightmare but went on to live a life devoted to God and to his family. He founded camps for troubled children and traveled the country telling others about the years he'd spent as a prisoner of war and how Jesus had rescued him. One sentence in the epilogue of the book lets me know that not only was Louie Zamperini courageous, faithful, and obedient, but he was also joyful. The author, Laura Hillenbrand, wrote, "He remained infectiously, incorrigibly cheerful. He once told a friend that the last time he could remember being angry was some forty years before."[4] He lived out the remainder of his life full of joy and died in 2014 at the age of ninety-seven.

Willie's Words on Being Joyful

When you meet the Robertsons, it won't take you long to know that we have a real spirit of joy that is 100 percent authentic. And I am not just talking about being *happy, happy, happy*, but real *joy, joy, joy*. That doesn't mean that there haven't been some real hard times, struggles, and many mistakes. But through it all, we know that being joyful is a deeper feeling we have and a better way to live.

Our joy comes first from our faith in God and His promises for us. Knowing and trusting whose we are and who we are shape our perspective, purpose, personality, and pursuit of being pleasant at all times and in all circumstances. Our faith gives us hope of something better to come; we know that no matter what happens on this earth, we are promised something even better.

As our children came into our lives, each was met with joy. John Luke came with a bit of a bobble by the doctor. (I seriously thought he was going to drop him. Perhaps the fact that he and I were watching the baseball World Series at the same time didn't help.) The joy with a firstborn is like no other. It's your first look at something you and your spouse made together.

When Sadie came along not much later . . . Ah, we had our boy and now our girl! Then our joy deepened even more when we welcomed Lil' Will into our family. He was just one month old when we got him. We felt so honored to get to be his parents and still count it as a gift. Then we had our sweet Bella. I have to admit, the first few months I didn't know if she would ever stop crying long enough to experience some joy. She finally did and now keeps us laughing with her quick wit and joyful spirit. The whole family got to welcome Rebecca when she joined the family at sixteen years of age. She came to us by way of Taiwan and couldn't even pronounce *joy*, but we knew from the start that she had it. Each of our children came in different ways, but we welcomed them all with the same joy.

I hope you're not thinking, *Yeah, I would have joy, too, if I were famous, had plenty of money, and all the things you guys have.* Well, let me stop you there. Our joy was there well before any of our success with the TV show. Korie and I did not have much money when we got married. I remember going to the grocery store as newlyweds with our envelope with a little cash in it. Whether to buy a two-dollar magazine would be a major conversation at the checkout counter. When we took over Duck Commander, we borrowed everything we could on credit cards and at the bank. And the decision to adopt Will didn't come because we could afford him—because we couldn't. It was just the right thing to do. As most people know, financial stress can steal your joy. Early on, we resolved that it would not steal ours.

Korie and I have worked hard to always show our children joy, even if there are stressors in our lives. We keep our faith at the front of our marriage and family life; that's how we know that the things we have are not what brings us joy. We know that if we lost all of our material possessions, we would still have joy. I'm always inspired by those who have dealt with major illness, death, or other losses yet still have joy.

Another important factor in our family is that we don't take ourselves too seriously. So many people do, and it steals their joy. They worry about this or that, and that worry can be a powerful joy-drainer. We learned from a young age to laugh at ourselves and laugh together. Being joyous is an attitude, a state of mind, but its foundation is in our hearts. I'm so glad that our TV show audience likes to laugh with us and at us. I think it's one of the reasons for our success. People need to laugh; it's healthy. So many people have let me know that even in the worst circumstances, they could turn on their TVs and just let go and laugh. When the media is so full of horrible things happening in this world, it's good to laugh. We can't let things on this earth paralyze us and steal our joy.

Hebrews 12:2 tells us this: "Run with perseverance the race marked out for us, fixing our eyes on Jesus, the pioneer and perfecter of faith. For the joy set before him he endured the cross, scorning its shame, and sat down at the right hand of the throne of God." Jesus had joy and also was willing to die an awful death knowing the joy that would come later. So no matter what circumstances we are in, the mere expectation of joy can give us joy.

I'm happy to say that when I look in my kids' eyes, I see joy. I'm sad to say that, as a former youth minister and college minister, I've seen many kids who don't have that joy in their eyes. They have been damaged either by parents, friends, divorce, sin, fear, or hopelessness. Life is way too short to lose our joy, and not seeing joy in a child is unacceptable. We need to forgive more, let our fears go, love more, and have fun! Go spread your joy to others.

FOURTEEN

LOYAL

For years Willie and I have been friends with Marcus Luttrell, the Lone Survivor. His love for and loyalty to his fellow SEALs are beyond match; they are a true family. We were also honored to have known Chris Kyle, the American Sniper. Our family has enormous respect for these American heroes whose loyalty to our country and to their fellow man provides the freedom that we all are blessed to have in our country today. I don't believe there is any greater evidence of the trait of loyalty than in men and women in our military. They deserve our utmost respect.

My grandfather, Papaw Howard, was a member of the United States Army Air Forces during World War II. Like Louie Zamperini, Papaw was a radio operator and a waist gunner. He was nineteen years old when he enlisted, which is the age of my John Luke at the time of this writing. (My heart skips a beat just thinking about it.) We are so blessed that my papaw left us his story in writing. He flew in a B-26, which was a medium bomber; Zamperini flew in a B-24. No plane promised a safe return, but the B-26 was nicknamed the "Widowmaker." Following is an excerpt from Papaw's account of one of his missions:

> This mission has been embedded in my mind until this day, fifty-six years later. What in the world was a nineteen-year-old boy who had never been hardly over two hundred miles from his birthplace on a forty-acre farm at Rocky Branch doing over a German city that he had never heard of and couldn't spell—or speak a word of their language? Well, I don't know, except the fact that someone

had to do the job, and my time had come. I only did what millions of other Americans and our Allied comrades did. We helped save the world from a tyrant named Adolph Hitler. Fortunately, I made it back home to tell my story. Many others did not, including our co-pilot, George Fisher, who lies in a graveyard in the Lorraine Cemetery in France along with 10,489 other comrades.

In that one paragraph my papaw exemplifies loyalty. What could cause a nineteen-year-old boy to leave his family and the safety of American soil to risk his life in battle? As Papaw said simply, "Someone had to do the job." Being loyal is "giving or showing firm and constant support or allegiance to a person or institution."[1] It's not backing away from doing whatever is needed to support someone or something. In this case, that was America and her freedom. Such loyalty goes beyond a simple definition, if that's possible. It's superhuman. Not everyone is asked to rise to such a level of loyalty, but to those who do, we continue to be grateful.

In our day-to-day lives (whether at work, school, home, or in our communities), loyalty has become a rare commodity. Many no longer expect it, and many might say that their dog is the most loyal friend they have. Dogs are often at the top of the list because it's in their nature to bond with their owners and show them undying love. There are plenty of stories about dogs that have risked their lives to save their owners. Dogs show up at the door with their tails wagging, welcoming us home. They rarely, if ever, question a request we make of them. In fact, they are eager to fetch anything thrown. Mark Twain wrote, "If you pick up a starving dog and make him prosperous, he will not bite you. This is the principal difference between a dog and a man."[2] I hope that's not true of most men.

Stick Together, No Matter What

We value loyalty in our family. When Willie and his brothers used to fight or weren't looking out for one another, Miss Kay loved to quote

1 John 4:20: "Whoever claims to love God yet hates a brother or sister is a liar. For whoever does not love their brother and sister, whom they have seen, cannot love God, whom they have not seen." She was trying to promote love and loyalty within the brothers, and I think she did a good job of this. All four brothers live on the same street with their families, and we love it that way. The Robertson brothers stick together no matter what, and the sisters-in-law do the same.

Miss Kay taught us another incredible lesson in love and loyalty when she forgave Phil and took him back after ten difficult years of marriage. One of my favorite memories of filming *Duck Dynasty* is the episode in which Phil and Miss Kay renewed their vows. It was beautiful for our children to be able to witness that and celebrate their grandparents' loyalty and commitment to marriage for richer and poorer, through good times and bad, in sickness and in health, and to see how their grandparents and our families have been so richly rewarded for their loyalty and commitment to one another.

LOYALTY REQUIRES COMMITMENT

Young children develop strong personal and emotional ties, but loyalty requires commitment, and commitment comes from those who are mature enough to honor their commitments. We can do many things to teach our children what loyalty is without ever using the word *loyal*. We can show our children the importance of looking out for their brothers and sisters. We can model for our children what loyalty looks like by being there in times of crisis for our church family as well as our physical family. We can show our children loyalty by remaining true to our marriage. We can display our support and allegiance to our country by standing when the Pledge of Allegiance is recited and by thanking veterans when we see them around town. As with all things, our actions will speak volumes to our children about loyalty. By instilling traits like responsibility, perseverance, honesty, and respect for others, we are giving our children the tools they'll need to be loyal friends, wives, husbands, and employees someday.

Willie's Words on Being Loyal

One thing that the Robertsons are known for is being loyal to our family. You might remember the national controversy over some things my father said. At one point there was discussion about removing him from the TV show. As a family we chose to stick together in support of Phil. Ultimately, we were able to continue filming our show as a family.

We grew up always sticking by each other no matter what. Sticking by each other doesn't mean we don't disagree or have arguments or, as kids, smack each other once in a while, but we were always loyal. I believe that knowing someone will be there for you in the ups and downs of life helps you develop many healthy life traits. Being loyal to my brothers was important, but being loyal to Korie is even more important. It's a daily lesson to our children and one any spouse shouldn't even have to think about. Korie and I will stand by each other in good times and bad times, and our children know that. At a very young age I was taught to be loyal to family, God, and country.

When Jase was about seventeen and I was about fifteen, he was seeing a girl who was coming out of another relationship. I guess my kids would describe it in today's terms as "it's complicated." This girl's former boyfriend was a real hothead, a football player, and not happy that his girl was seeing Jase. He confronted Jase and, in the heat of the moment, he punched him. Jase did not retaliate and actually used the situation to try and preach to him. Now, I was a pretty spiritual guy myself, but no one was going to punch my brother and get away with it. I jumped in the car with my friends and went looking for this guy.

I didn't care that he was twice my size. I was going to let him know that anyone punching my family was going to get a visit from me. Luckily for him, and probably luckier for me, I didn't find him. Jase talked me out of it and actually taught me a lesson on turning the other cheek—literally.

Now, why was I so willing to stick up and potentially get leveled for the guy who whaled on me hundreds of times growing up? The answer is loyalty. I was going to stand by Jase, no matter what. I don't advocate fighting or punching or retaliating, but I do want my kids to stick up for one another, to protect one another, and to be loyal to one another. I want them to be loyal to us as parents even though we discipline them, bug them to do homework, and drive them crazy by trying to guide them in life—just as we stay loyal to them no matter how they act at times. We love them, and our decision to be loyal to them will not change. To end the story of the angry ex-boyfriend, I'm happy to announce that he is now a godly guy with a great family, and we are all friends.

Perhaps the best lesson I saw on loyalty came from watching my mom as she remained loyal to my dad even though she had every right not to. I was too young at the time to fully understand the impact this would have on our family, but I now know her loyalty saved us all. We all received the benefits from that lesson: me, my brothers, our wives, our children, our children's children, and generations to come. That act of loyalty impacted our family but also went on to impact our culture and people all over the world. Being loyal even when it's not deserved is the most impressive. Kay was displaying what she had learned from Jesus and applying it to Phil. Jase applied teachings from Jesus as well to deal with a hotheaded ex-boyfriend. Korie displays loyalty to me constantly even when I don't deserve it. Her parents have shown loyalty to each other for more than forty years. All of my children have great examples of loyalty, and I pray they'll display that in their lives.

FIFTEEN

HUMBLE

If I were to ask a group of modern parents whether they want their children to have feelings of insignificance, I'm pretty sure that most of them would shake their heads and shout, "No!" But if I were to ask the same parents whether they wanted their children to be humble, they would respond, "Yes, of course." Humility seems to be an old-fashioned concept, but it's one I believe still has merit.

Humility is having or showing a modest or low estimate of one's own importance. *What?* you're thinking. *That's crazy. I love humble people, but I don't want my child to have a low estimate of his own importance.* And I would ask, why not? Romans 12:3 clearly says, "Do not think of yourself more highly than you ought, but rather think of yourself with sober judgment, in accordance with the faith God has distributed to each of you."

Yes, I get that, you're thinking, *but according to the latest magazine article I read, healthy self-esteem will help my children resist negative pressure in the world. They'll be happier and live a better life.* Now we're all confused.

A LESSON IN HUMILITY

My mom taught me a quick lesson in humility that I've never forgotten. I was in middle school, had started wearing makeup, and had suddenly gotten really self-conscious about my appearance. I didn't go anywhere without my pink lip gloss, my Cover Girl face powder, and my hair teased and sprayed just so (it was the '80s—don't judge). We were on a road trip, and I had slept in and just climbed into the car without going through my hour-long process of getting ready. We stopped at a gas station, and I needed to go to the bathroom, but I was not about to get out of the van and let other people see me like that. I'm not sure what I planned on doing—holding it for the entire five-hour drive? But I was holding firm; no way was I going in there.

I think at this point, Mom had had enough. She said, "You must think really highly of yourself if you think everyone else is paying that much attention to you to worry about whether you have lipstick on and your hair sprayed."

What? This was not about me thinking highly of myself; this was about me being self-conscious, or so I thought. My mom went on to tell me that no one else was worried about me or what I looked like, and that I just needed to get over myself. She pointed out that most people are too busy thinking about themselves to worry about what anyone else looks like or is doing, and for me to think other people were looking at me that closely was actually a form of thinking too highly of myself.

That struck me hard, and I remember it to this day. I resolved then not to worry so much about how I look or the little things that we think other people are noticing about us, because the truth is, they most likely are not. Of course I like to look nice when I go out in public. I try to look my best when I'm filming the show or doing a red-carpet event. But on many days, I go out with little or no makeup on and my hair in a messy bun. Mom was right—worrying too much about how I look and whether people are judging me is a way of thinking too highly of myself. I don't want to be that person.

One day shortly after *Duck Dynasty* first started, I stopped by Walmart after playing a round of tennis. I know some people who look cute as a button after working out or playing sports, but I'm not one of those people. Louisiana is hot in the summertime, and when I get hot playing tennis, I'll have a red face for an hour afterward. Plus, my hair was back in a ponytail, and frizzies were sticking out. I didn't think a thing about it until I was in the parking lot in Walmart and someone asked to take a picture with me. I said, "Yes, of course."

Then she looked at me and said, "Oh, are you sure it's okay with your hair like that?"

I had to laugh. I said, "I don't mind, go ahead." No telling what that picture looked like, but if Mom hadn't taught me that lesson in middle school, I might have said no to that picture or not even gone to the store until I had gone home, showered, and made up my face. If I'd not had that lesson in middle school, life would not be nearly as much fun, having to always worry about looking perfect before going out in public.

Humility, Not Self-Esteem

Our topic of humility must also include a discussion of self-esteem. My grandmother, Mamaw Jo Shackelford, who is very wise, tells me that the term *self-esteem* didn't even exist when she was growing up. Neither did it exist when she was raising her children. So the idea of having healthy self-esteem is relativity new in child rearing. In fact, Mamaw Jo says that if she got a new dress and came out to show the family, her grandmother might have told her that it was pretty, but she would definitely have followed the compliment with the caution, "Pretty is as pretty does." The notion that one's worth was not to be wrapped up in one's appearance was the accepted wisdom of the time. Somewhere in the 1960s, the term *self-esteem* began to move beyond the psychology books and into mainstream language. *Self-concept* had been studied for many years prior, but it and its brother, *self-esteem*, were not terms used by common folks. I'm hoping and praying that we as a country have finally figured out that a trophy and a high five for every kid is not the path to healthy self-esteem.

The term *self-esteem* implies that we esteem ourselves, which is contrary to the biblical view of our importance, as noted in the earlier verses of Scripture. The Bible offers many more verses and examples that show us that esteeming ourselves is not on God's roadmap to a smoother life. (Check out Numbers 20, where Moses struck the rock instead of speaking to it as God had commanded. When Moses decided to take matters into his own hands, it didn't work out too well for him.)

The word *esteem* means "respect and admiration."[1] In the past I've been okay with using the phrase *self-respect* instead of *self-esteem*. However, when I looked up the definition of *respect*, it said "to admire." Then the definition went further, saying "a deep admiration for someone or something elicited by their abilities, qualities, or achievements."[2] In other words, it's okay to admire yourself if your ability warrants. Hmm . . . I'm not sure that's what we're after either.

Self-esteem can be a tricky subject, but there is nothing tricky about the fact that God's word calls us to be humble. Ephesians 4:2 tells us, "Be completely humble and gentle; be patient, bearing with one another in love." And again in 1 Peter 3:8 we read, "Finally, all of you, be like-minded, be sympathetic, love one another, be compassionate and humble." No matter what all the books out there tell us about building our kids' self-esteem, the One who created us reminds us that humility should be our goal.

Willie's Words on Being Humble

Teaching humility to children can be very difficult. We humans come into this world thinking we are at the center of it. Just watch a toddler for a few minutes. When his toy is taken away, he'll immediately bristle. As Korie mentioned earlier, *my* and *mine* are two of the first words most children say. Then they go from saying "mine" to using *I* in most of their sentences. "I want." "I don't want." "I don't like." This is natural for a time, but not for long. As soon as we hear those signs of "it's all about me," it's time to start teaching kids that it really isn't. When we fail to do this, the result is a spoiled child who thinks the world revolves around him or her. That type of child becomes an adult with the potential of self-destructing. I want my children to have good qualities and feel good about themselves, but I want others to point that out. I don't want my kids bragging about themselves because they feel they are better than anyone else or deserve more than anyone else.

When Sadie was competing on *Dancing with the Stars*, Korie and I heard the most wonderful things about her. She had every opportunity to think she was a pretty big deal. I was so proud to see her achieve so much at a young age, but I was most impressed with her ability to stay humble. During that same time our daughter Bella was competing in a cheer competition in Memphis. Up until that point in her life, Bella had not really done many sports, so this was a big deal for her. It was a busy time for our family. We were traveling to Los Angeles every weekend and filming the TV show, but the family also loaded up and went to see Bella perform in Memphis. I was just as proud of Bella as I was of Sadie. And Sadie was proud of Bella too. When siblings can cheer one another on no matter how big the platform, it teaches them to get out of themselves and focus on others and what others are doing.

We all want our kids to have pride in themselves, win a few ribbons and trophies, and be confident, but we also want them to stay humble. That sounds hard, doesn't it? But there are some simple things you can do to help your children stay humble. I learned these from my parents. One thing is to stress with your children that everyone has his or her own way of being great, but no one is more important than anyone else. Another thing is to show your children that it's okay to have pride in a job well done, but it's also important to be able to recognize when other people have done a job well. These simple truths can be taught to kids of all ages.

First and foremost, they have to see the pride and humility in you, their parents. Dad needs to brag on Mom, and Mom needs to brag on Dad. This shows children that Mom and Dad value each other and that everyone's work is important. When parents argue over who does something better, they are show-ing children the opposite of humility. Traits we want our chil-dren to have must be seen in us, their parents.

Being humble starts with thinking of others; it's taking pride in what we do but not thinking we're the most important per-son. This is the whole message of the birth and death of Jesus. Philippians 2:8 says that Jesus "humbled himself by being obe-dient to death—even death on a cross!" The ultimate example of humility was taught by our Lord. Keeping this thought first in our minds will help us be more humble while on this earth.

PART THREE

HOW TO PARENT KIDS OF CHARACTER

MAKING IT WORK

Now that we've contemplated the important traits we want to instill in our children, it's time to discuss how we are going to go about actually doing it.

I had a conversation with a young man once who was telling me about how he grew up in the church and then left it for a while and lived a life away from God, full of partying, drugs, and alcohol. Growing up he had sung in the choir and been at the church building with his family every time the doors were open. I asked him, "Why do you think you abandoned your faith for a while?" His answer was very insightful, and one I think all of us parents need to hear. He said, "My parents and the people at our church said they valued the things God values, but they lived their lives like they valued the things of the world." He went on to tell me that in Bible class he was taught things such as the importance of taking care of the poor and that earthly riches and outer beauty don't matter, but through the actions of the adults in his world, he was taught exactly the opposite. He saw that the adults in his life were consumed with their jobs, homes, cars, and looks. Their lives didn't match their words and their children noticed.

You'll see that most of the remaining chapters start with the verb *be*. We can't just think about what we want for our kids. We can't just hope they are getting it through the lessons in Bible class. In the end it comes down to living these traits ourselves and doing things on a daily basis that imprint these values onto our children's hearts and minds. It will take us *being* kind and strong and loving and compassionate. It requires giving our children consistent training, including both discipline and love, and living the life God intended for us confidently, intentionally, and creatively.

There will be things we will have to change within ourselves if we want to see them in our children. As you know, parenting is so much more than taking care of basic needs of food, shelter, and clothing. The job of parenting never goes away—it involves constant learning, growing, maturing, being there, being in the moment, and even being all the things you want your children to be. It's not easy, but it is all worth every single second.

SIXTEEN

BE CONFIDENT

One of the most important pieces of parenting advice I got from my mom (and she got it from her mom) is to be a confident parent. With conflicting advice from numerous parenting "experts" these days, it can be easy to question your parenting skills. In fact, not being sure of yourself seems to be fashionable in our current culture. After all, who wants to appear as if they have all the answers? Today's parents are more likely to talk and act as if they don't have a clue about how to parent their children. They shrug their shoulders as their children run through a store or talk disrespectfully to them. They say, "I give up," as their children continue to behave in a way they've been told not to.

At one time in parenting history, parents knew exactly how to raise children; they simply did what their parents did. Back then aunts, uncles, grandparents, and teachers were all trusted adults who had a part in raising a child, and everyone mostly agreed as to what was best for the child. What the teacher said at school was reinforced at home and vice versa. If a child spoke in a disrespectful way, not one adult questioned how to handle that child. If a child ran through a store, not one adult wondered how to contain him or her. The roles of adults and children were never in question. Children listened to adults and, except for times of mischievous behavior, did as they were told. Adults, in turn, had the assurance that they were entrusted with guiding any children in their path with confidence and love.

Now, I'm not saying that all parents in the past were good. You may have been raised in a home that caused you some pain. You might be doing all you can *not* to do the same things your parents did. If that's true, I applaud you and encourage you in your effort to begin a new, more positive legacy in your family. My point here is that with all of the parenting books, blogs, and theories out there (I realize that I'm contributing to this phenomenon by writing this book but hopefully not in a bad way), it can make us question *everything* we do. I believe that's part of the problem with our parenting.

The Owner's Manual for Kids—the Bible

For the past forty or fifty years, doctors, child psychologists, day-care workers, teachers, counselors, preachers, parents with lots of kids, and now even I have decided to share parenting tips and techniques. One of my favorite child experts is John Rosemond. I have had the pleasure of hearing John Rosemond speak on several occasions, and he often refers to the parenting book phenomenon as the "Tower of Parent-Babble." He is certainly right![1] As of this writing, when I typed in the word *parenting* on Amazon.com, it brought up more than 108,000 books. No wonder we're a nation of confused parents! I saw books on a wide range of topics, including how to be the playful parent, how to deal with an explosive child, and how to make it through parenting without screaming.

Certainly there is a lot of great information out there, but none of it is good if it causes you to second-guess everything you do as a parent. This plethora of parenting books can lead one to think that good parenting is nearly impossible. But being a good parent is really pretty simple. I'm not saying it's easy, but I am saying that it's not as difficult as some of today's parenting experts would lead you to believe. You can be confident of this: God has given you the ability to raise the children He has given you, and He has provided you with the best parenting book on the market: the Bible.

I've heard it said many times that children don't come with an owner's manual, but they really do. The Bible has all the instructions we need to raise strong and kind children because every biblical truth is a parenting tip. Consider this: Eve didn't have a mom to go to for advice when Cain was colicky, when he threw temper tantrums, or when he was jealous of the new baby, Abel. She certainly didn't have a hundred thousand parenting books to choose from, yet she managed to raise her children. I know what you're thinking. Her kids were far from perfect. You're right. They had some major problems (Gen. 4:8). And Eve wasn't perfect either. She made a major mistake (Gen. 3:6). I love that God gives example after example of not-so-perfect parents and children for us to examine and study as we navigate our earthly journey. If we were perfect, we wouldn't need Him!

So if you are a brand-new mom with a perfect baby, I've got news for you: it won't last long. Being perfect parents and raising perfect children should never be our goal. Raising children who believe in a perfect God is.

CONFIDENCE IN PARENTING

Always remember, you don't have to be a perfect parent, but it does help to be confident. In some ways children are like horses; they can sense weakness.

Sadie was five years old when a movie about a wild horse that couldn't be tamed, *Spirit: Stallion of the Cimarron*, was in theaters. I decided to take all of the kids to the movie, which was a feat in itself. John Luke was six, Sadie was five, Will was one, and Bella was a newborn. We had just walked into the movie theater when Sadie realized that she'd left her stuffed animal in the car. She loved her bear and had planned on snuggling with it while she watched the movie. Sadie was usually a blast to be around; she was always making us laugh and had a way about her that lit up a room. But she had a stubborn streak that I was trying to tame at the time. Needless to say, she was not happy about leaving her bear and begged me to go back to the car to get it. Not a simple request for a mom with four little kids and a giant diaper bag. I told her no, she would be fine without it.

Sadie changed from being happy about going to the movie to extremely unhappy. She pouted and whined through all the previews and the beginning of the movie. I warned her that pouting and whining wouldn't change my mind and would only ruin her enjoyment of the movie, but at five years of age, she was not convinced by this reasoning. I was confident that no permanent damage would come from Sadie not having her bear for two hours during a movie, so I stuck to my guns. Still, she continued to pout.

Soon the movie began, and the story of taming the wild horse began to develop. I remember laughing to myself in that dark theater, thinking, *Sadie is kind of like that wild horse that needs to be tamed.* Now don't misunderstand me; I never want to break my children's spirits, but there are times when it is necessary to tame their strong wills. That requires a mom who is confident that she knows better than her children.

When parents or other adults are unsure of their actions, when they constantly second-guess or change their decisions based on their children's actions or reactions or the latest book or blog, children will sense weakness. They'll go on pouting or whining for as long as they think it will take for you to break. That day, when Sadie learned that her pouting and whining would not break me, she eventually wiped the frown off her face and enjoyed the movie. And the next time, it didn't take her nearly as long to accept that no means no.

When managing a horse, a confident rider lets the horse know that he is in control. Thus, the horse feels safe and secure with his rider. He learns to trust the rider, and the horse is a happy horse. In the same way, children learn to trust and depend on a confident parent. Confident parenting creates secure children. Children who do not have confident parents spend their time second-guessing what is expected of them, whereas children with moms and dads who make decisions with confidence will grow to feel safe and secure.

CONFIDENT PARENTING OF UNIQUE PERSONALITIES

Our children are not perfect, but they know that when we ask them to clean their rooms, finish their homework, take out the trash, or do anything else, we expect them to do it. These are examples of task-oriented responsibilities, but in the same way, our children have expectations of us. They don't doubt that their parents love them and love each other; they're confident that we'll make decisions based on our faith in God and His Word; they are certain that we'll feed them, clothe them, and meet their physical needs; they never doubt that we always have their best interests at heart. Because Willie and I have worked to be confident parents, our children have learned to trust their parents both in what we expect from them and what they can expect from us, and they have become confident kids.

Undoubtedly all your children will have unique personalities. That's God's great secret for keeping us humble and seeking Him. If Willie and I had stopped with John Luke and Sadie, we might have gone to our graves thinking parenting was easy. John Luke and Sadie were twenty months apart. There was just enough time for me to get my bearings as the mother of a toddler and get ready for a newborn again. Not so when Will and Bella came along. God has a great sense of humor, as we were soon to find out.

We adopted Will in December 2001 when he was five weeks old and then went on a fun-filled, surprise (to me) trip to Cancun for our tenth anniversary in January 2002. I came back pregnant with Bella (another surprise to me), who was born in September 2002. Some people say that having children so close together—just ten months apart for Will and Bella—is harder than having twins. I've never had twins, so I don't know what to compare it to, but I will admit that life was crazy for a couple of years.

Will wasn't walking yet when Bella was born, so I constantly had a baby on each hip. Even when Will started walking, I usually chose to carry him because if I'd put him down, I never would've been able to catch up with him. Those two were such a handful that we nicknamed them Destructo 1 and Destructo 2. My mom said that Will would open a window and Bella would climb out. There were days when I thought I just might climb out the window myself and stay out there for a while. But here's what I learned.

Although Will's and Bella's personalities were different from John Luke's and Sadie's—and I now had four little ones to tend to rather than two—it didn't change what Willie and I did as parents. Our parenting principles stayed the same even though our children's personalities and circumstances were vastly different. Having two that close in age caused me to have to be more diligent—more confident.

I remember telling Willie that people at church probably thought that I had ADD because I couldn't concentrate on a conversation without my eyes darting around to keep an eyeball on all of my children. Being confident isn't always easy, and it's rarely convenient, but it's always necessary. So even when we were at church or at a grocery store or restaurant with others watching us, we couldn't waver in what we did to train our children. We had to remain confident in the knowledge that God had given us these children. He had entrusted us to show them His love and to raise them up in the way they should go.

I'll never forget walking into the kitchen early one morning to find our curly-headed Will on the kitchen counter. Dressed in his footed pajamas, he had pushed the kitchen chair over to the cabinet to provide the first step up in his quest for cereal and cookies. Bella was waiting below for the food Will threw down to her eager hands. (We truly believe that if we had left them at home alone, they would have figured out how to survive.)

With two children so close in age, one is often more cautious than the other, but not so with Will and Bella. They both were adventurous and determined, and they thought they could conquer the world. If any kids needed a confident mom and dad, it was these two, and they challenged my confidence plenty.

Willie and I repeatedly took Will down from the cabinet and told him not to get up there. We were not deterred by the fact that he ignored us and did it again and again. When a child doesn't do what a parent says to do, that's not the time to stop saying it; it's time to stand firm and be even more consistent. When results come slowly, it's easy for parents to think that what they're doing isn't working. We're all used to quick results in our microwave-oven society. But remind yourself how long God had to stick to His guns with the Israelites and many others in the Bible.

The Israelites had a long history of cycles of obedience followed by rebellion followed by obedience. Surely God grew tired of telling His chosen people to stop what they were doing. But God didn't tire, and He didn't quit. Obviously, God isn't dependent on quick results. No extra credit is given to parents who succeed in getting their kids to change their behavior the first time. Being consistent and confident will ultimately result in changed behavior.

I have a few more Will stories for you, and I know that some of you will relate to them. I'm not the only one who had a challenging toddler! In fact, Will was such a handful that I used to have to warn babysitters that he could sense weakness a mile away, and if they didn't get their bluff in early, he would walk all over them. By the time I started leaving the youngest two with sitters, Will had learned to behave for me (except when he sensed I was distracted taking care of one of the other kids) because he knew I wasn't going to let him get away with disobedience, and he knew Willie certainly wouldn't put up with any nonsense. But if he sensed weakness in the person in charge, he was a mess.

When Willie went on hunting trips, I noticed Will's behavior worsened the longer Willie was away. Will's strong will (maybe that's why his name is Will) needed a strong presence. I also observed that he wouldn't do anything he was told to do unless he knew there would be an immediate consequence for disobedience. He was always putting this to the test. Everything I asked him to do had to be followed with an "or else." "Put your shoes on or you won't get to go outside." "Bring me those scissors or you'll have to sit in time-out." "Stop hitting Bella or you'll have to go to your room . . ." I couldn't just say, "Put down that pen." He simply would not do it. Yes, he was busy *and* stubborn. Corralling and teaching him and each of our children took a lot of hard work that involved confident, consistent discipline and *prayer*. And still does!

When Will was nearly three years old, I dropped John Luke and Sadie off for their first day of school at Ouachita Christian School (OCS). Will and Bella were with me, and Will started saying that he was going to school. I soon realized that Will thought he was going to be staying at school that day as well, so I explained to him that he wasn't old enough to go this year. He was so disappointed. It was adorable. He was a very smart and verbal child, so I thought, *This kid needs some type of school to go to.* I found him a sweet Montessori school that was exactly what he needed. The teachers had been teaching for a long time; they were kind but authoritative. The school program had a great mix of structure and free play for his three-year-old mind.

Will thrived in this environment; he loved it, and I loved that he loved it. The only struggle was on the playground, which was covered with tiny pebbles. On a few occasions the teacher told me that she had a difficult time getting him to leave the pebbles on the playground; he seemed determined to throw them. I disciplined him about this, but I secretly thought that the temptation was just too big—a playground full of thousands of tiny rocks! Wouldn't most three-year-old boys feel the urge to throw a rock from time to time? All in all, Will's first year of preschool was a great experience.

The next year, I enrolled him in the preschool program at OCS. He was so excited, and so was I. This meant that our three oldest kids would be at the same school. The previous year, John Luke and Sadie were at OCS every day from 8:00 a.m. to 3:00 p.m., Will was at the Montessori school from 9:00 a.m. to noon, and Bella went to a Mother's Day Out program two days a week from 9:00 a.m. to 2:00 p.m. Whew! With all the drop-offs and pick-ups, it hardly seemed worth it; but Will loved school, and he was an active boy at home, so I survived the year with lots of time in the car. Still, having just two different destinations was going to be much easier for me.

At orientation for Will's upcoming school year at OCS, I noticed that his new teacher seemed very sweet, but it was her first year teaching. Knowing Will's propensity to sense weakness and take advantage of the situation, I was nervous. I suspected that his new teacher's inexperience and sweet demeanor might not be right for Will. Sure enough, when I picked him up from the first day of school, I learned that he'd already made a trip to the principal's office! In no way did I blame his teacher; Will was a handful. At home we talked about his behavior and about how he was going to mind his teacher the next day. But day after day, Will would be in time-out at school or would have to pull a strip (kids start the day with a certain number of strips, then pull one each time they need to be corrected) or stay inside at recess.

After three weeks of this repeated behavior and discipline at home and school, Will didn't like school anymore. It was alarming to see this in our kid who, just a year before, had begged to go to school. We made the decision to pull him out and let him attend another preschool program that John Luke and Sadie had attended when they were younger. I felt confident in this decision because I knew the teacher there. She was a sweet, older woman who had been teaching kids for a long time. She had, no doubt, seen it all. Will seemed to sense her confidence right off the bat, and it didn't take him long to go back to loving school. This teacher often told me how much she loved Will and that she thought he had the sweetest heart. She said he was very smart but sometimes got a little overactive (you think?). She said that she had to keep an eye on him and a hand on his hand to make sure he was doing what he was supposed to do. She knew exactly what Will needed.

Because of his personality, Will required confident, consistent authority. As I write this, I'm reminded that he was only four. He was still in his early formative years, and I'm grateful to have found a teacher with such wisdom to help me mold and shape our little man. Under this teacher's careful watch, Will thrived that year. He went on to big school at OCS the next year and did great. I'm not saying there weren't times in his early years when he pulled a strip, but, thankfully, he made no more trips to the principal's office.

Will still loves school. He loves his teachers as much as he loves his friends. Again, I don't blame his first teacher. If Will had been my first child, he surely would have sensed fear and, possibly, panic in me as well. I'm thankful God chose to give me Will as a third child. Will's story underscores the need for strong, confident adults to lead our children. Without that, Will became unhappy. Confident adults breathe life into children. Children feel safe when they know that someone will be there to rein them in when necessary.

CONFIDENCE IN GOD

I'm sure you can see why I'm *extremely* sympathetic to God when I read about His patience with and love for the Israelites. I know He understands what I've gone through as a parent. We've survived the toddler years, and I miss the sweet days of watching those two cuties snuggled up watching cartoons in the mornings or reading books with them in the bed at night. Now Will is a confident teen and Bella a confident preteen. They're both happy and secure. I have no doubts that we'll still face some parenting challenges, but we'll face them with confidence that God will give us what we need.

Even if you begin to doubt yourself as a parent, never doubt God. Have confidence that He will lead and guide you. Continue to pray for wisdom, and put your children in His hands. Tell God the traits that you're working to instill in your children, and know that He is working in their lives in an even bigger way than you are. Then go out there with the confidence that comes from knowing that when God is for you, no one can be against you.

Willie's Words on Being Confident

I still remember when Korie came to me and said, "You have to deal with these kids." Our children were young, and she had just gone through one of those days. She felt like she had done all she could do, and they still needed some discipline. I remember thinking, *I just got home. Now I have to be the bad guy.* But I knew I had a job to do. Yes, I had at been at work all day trying to provide for my family. Yes, I was tired. Yes, I just wanted to come home and wrestle with my kids and, yes, I wanted everyone to just be happy. But I still had a job to do.

On that particular day Korie had just spent all day working too. She had put in another day of loving and nurturing our children and training them to be good people. She had cooked for them, put up their toys, and read them stories. Even though she had filled the day with kindness toward them, they were rebelling. They were young and still in the training stage. They were at an age when rebelling comes pretty natural. They didn't yet have the maturity to see the big picture or to realize some level of appreciativeness. They were simply being disobedient to their mother and were intent on punching each other. This was not the time for analysis; it was the time for action. I had to let them know that what they were doing wasn't going to work.

That day is a few years in the past, but this is how Korie and I still deal with our children: if Korie tells one of the kids that Dad will deal with them later, they know it's serious. I don't want you to think Korie is some sort of June Cleaver character who wears her pearls while she does housework and doesn't want to deal with problems. Korie works hard, both at our company and at home, and is a strong leader for our children. Most of the time, she handles discipline issues before they ever get to me. But there are those times when she needs reinforcement, when she needs to let the situation yield to another level of strength, and that's Dad. This speaks to a healthy relationship. Trust and teamwork from two loving parents will help kids become the best they can be. There is a godly principle of two being stronger than one, and this is a perfect example of that principle. When a child looks up and realizes that Mom and Dad are always on the same page, the idea of misbehaving isn't so attractive anymore.

I know that the job that I go to each day to support my

family is important, but my first job is helping my kids become good people. I realized that day—and still know—that the buck stops with me. I'm the first and last line of defense for making them behave properly. This job requires a confident parent. There's no time to cry or be buddy-buddy. I'm not talking about a confidence that says you're bigger or stronger. I'm talking about having the kind of confidence that lets your kids know that you're the one in charge.

Part of my job as a dad is to create a healthy fear in my kids that tells them they must behave and be obedient. If I show signs of weakness, it will undermine our ultimate goal as parents and open them up to problems with others in authority positions. As the dad, I also represent the teacher they would someday deal with, the police officer they might encounter, or their future employer. It isn't the fun part of my dad job, but it is the job that I have been called to do.

SEVENTEEN

BE CONSISTENT

I can't believe I'm writing a chapter about consistency because in most areas of my life, consistency is not my strong suit. Although I hate to speak for Willie, since I'm the one writing this, I'll go ahead and tell you: it's not his either. I used to define our marriage like this: if I didn't like something he was doing, I'd just wait a few days, and it would change.

As we've gotten older, I think we're settling in our ways a little, but for the most part, Willie and I don't do the same thing two days in a row—ever. I don't even get ready the same way in the morning. Some days when I'm putting on my makeup, I do my eyes first. Sometimes I put my lipstick on right when I look in the mirror just because I feel like it. Sometimes I get dressed and then blow-dry my hair; sometimes I stay in my robe till the last possible minute and then throw my clothes on and head out the door. Maybe everyone changes their morning routine every day, but I would guess that a lot of you reading this have lives that are a little more predictable than the ones we live.

Our work schedule couldn't be more different on a day-to-day basis. A typical week may look something like this: Monday meetings in the office all day, Tuesday filming a redneck waterpark for *Duck Dynasty*, Wednesday a photo shoot for our clothing boutique, Duck and Dressing, Thursday in pajamas all day working from home on my book, Friday hopping a plane to New York City for a press tour. And then the next week everything changes. I know all of us are busy, so I don't tell you this to say how busy my life is, only to say that for the most part, consistency is just not our thing.

CONSISTENCY DEPENDS ON PERSONALITY

A lot of parenting books encourage you to have a consistent nap time, bath time, and bottle and bedtime routine. For me, those things come under the category of whatever works for you and your family. If you're the kind of person who likes schedules and routines, go for it. If you're not, don't stress about this.

Before John Luke was born, I read a book claiming it could teach you to train your baby to sleep through the night in eight weeks or less. As a first-time mom, I was all in. I read the book and committed to doing everything it said. Of course, I wanted my baby to sleep through the night as quickly as possible, so I was willing to follow this book step by step. The steps were as follows: feed your baby every three hours on the dot; even if your baby is crying, don't give in and feed him early; put your baby in his crib an hour and a half after the last feeding regardless of whether he is sleepy; let your baby cry until he falls asleep to train him that it's bedtime; don't hold your baby when he is sleeping . . . and on and on.

Needless to say, this mama, who doesn't even put her clothes on the same way every day, ended up at church one Wednesday night bawling her eyes out. I'll never forget someone coming up to me and asking, "Aw, do you have the baby blues?" I said through my tears, "I do not have the baby blues. My baby just won't eat when he's supposed to." John Luke was not fitting into my schedule; but, more than that, this schedule that I had created for John Luke wasn't fitting into my life. I like flexibility and spontaneity, and it turns out, John Luke does too. This rigid schedule allowed no time for spontaneity, and it was sucking all of the fun out of being a first-time mom. Plus, I was not about to just put my newborn in the bed and let him cry it out. I had given up on that one the first day in.

If you're a planner who loves a date book and a schedule, this type of baby raising is perfect for you, but for me, it was stifling, exhausting, and no fun. Right after that crying spell at church, I decided to do what I felt was right for my baby and me. After I made that major decision, life began to level out. While I'm sure this book has helped many new moms, it just wasn't for me. With each new baby, I learned more and began to trust my own instincts.

I also learned that a schedule does work for some babies. Our Will is still the first to go to bed at night and the first to wake up. He and Sadie tended to fall into a schedule more naturally. I still didn't adhere to a strict schedule with them, and many times they would just fall asleep wherever we were—a restaurant, a friend's house, or a ball game. Children are amazingly resilient, and given the opportunity, they will adapt to whatever situation they are in.

Be Consistent in Discipline

As inconsistent as Willie and I are in other areas of our life, one thing we committed to being consistent about was disciplining our children. To me, this is where consistency is most needed. When our kids were babies, we determined that we would not be parents who disciplined our kids one day and then were too tired the next day to get out of the chair to stop them from getting away with the thing we had just disciplined them for a day earlier. This is not fair to kids and will not produce the results anyone wants in their children. Kids will test the limits, and if they know that they can sometimes get away with bad behavior, they'll keep on trying. It's like gambling or buying a lottery ticket. If you sometimes win, you're going to keep playing.

Four Reasons Parents Are Not Consistent in Discipline

Besides just not wanting to get the job done, there are four reasons I see that keep parents from being consistent disciplinarians.

Fatigue

This first one, fatigue, is understandable because, goodness knows, we all suffer from it. After your two-year-old gets out of bed fifteen times, you will be tempted to give him the juice he wants—and anything else you can find. But don't give in. By returning him to bed with a kind but confident voice, you are letting him know that you are the one in authority. Trust me. Eventually there will be a payoff.

When John Luke was a baby, I would take him to the health club with me and put him in the nursery while I worked out. It was a great time for me to take care of myself a little, and the girl who worked the nursery was as sweet as she could be. John Luke did great there for a while, happily crawling around and playing with toys that were different from the ones he had at home. However, all babies seem to go through a stage where only mama will do. It hit my babies at around nine months to a year old. In this phase even other family members they have previously lunged for sometimes will not fit the bill; they want Mama—all day, every day. Well, John Luke hit this phase, and he began to cry when I dropped him off at the nursery. It was tempting to just give up. It took effort to get dressed, get bags packed, and get out the door in the morning for a workout, and then it seemed like a waste of time when I just had to turn around and go home. But I knew John Luke needed to get past this, and an hour-long workout three days a week was something this mama needed. Nothing bad was happening to him while he was in there. The same sweet girl he'd been happy to go with for months was keeping him. This was just a phase he was going through, so I continued to go to the health club and attempted to leave him in the nursery.

I would sweetly kiss him and tell him that he'd be just fine as I pried his arms from around my neck and passed him off to the babysitter before calmly walking out the door. While I said earlier I was not down with leaving my newborn to cry himself to sleep in his crib, by the time my babies were ten months old, I knew there were times when they were just going to have to cry it out. The only problem was, the health club had a policy that if a baby cried for more than ten minutes, the childcare worker was to intercom the parent. In ten minutes I would have barely gotten up the stairs and onto the treadmill, and I'd hear my name over the intercom. John Luke was just a baby, but he knew that if he cried long enough, they would call me, and I'd come get him.

This happened a few times until one day, there were no other babies in the nursery. So I asked the girl if she would mind keeping him a little longer than the allotted ten minutes just to see if John Luke would get past it. Sure enough, I got an entire forty-five-minute workout in with no call. When I went to pick him up, he was smiling and playing on the floor. I asked the babysitter how long he had cried and she said only about fifteen minutes. Once the normal ten minutes had passed, John Luke realized that it wasn't working and that he might as well make the best of it.

The next time I went to work out, he still cried when I dropped him off, but the babysitter assured me that she would wait it out. Once again it took about fifteen minutes, and the worst was over. On my next visit he cried only about five minutes. After that it wasn't long before there were no more tears at drop-off. Once again John Luke was a happy baby in the nursery. You see, consistency works both ways: If a child consistently gets what he wants by crying, whining, or complaining, then he will consistently cry, whine, or complain until he gets it. If he doesn't, then he'll likely learn it's not worth the effort.

Kid Fascination

Have you seen parents who are so fascinated with their kids that they allow them to make everyone else's life miserable? Oddly enough, I've seen some very mild-mannered parents produce a little firecracker. While the parents find this child completely fascinating, the rest of the world may not think she's quite so cute. Don't be so fascinated with your kids that you can't see when they need a firm hand to control them. We've all seen parents who think it's just adorable that their kid loves to bang on everything. Will was like this, and now he's amazing on the drums. He was also a squealer, and now he has a great singing voice.

Will's banging on his high chair or pots and pans or whatever he could find and squealing really didn't bother me at all. He had good rhythm, even as a baby, so I allowed him to bang away when we were at home. Willie's really loud, too, so we don't mind a noisy house. I realized, however, that other people probably wouldn't appreciate his banging and squealing like we did, so I did my best to keep this contained when we were in public. I always made sure to sit by him when we were out to eat or at church so I could keep this behavior under control, and I was careful to move all of the silverware beyond his reach. In the car on the way to a public place, we would discuss that we must be respectful of others and not be as loud as we might be at home. While Will's banging and squealing were something we saw as future talents, we couldn't be so enamored of our little child prodigy that we allowed him to take over an entire restaurant.

One of the strangest things I've seen that goes along with this idea of kid fascination is those shoes parents put on their babies that make a loud squeak every step they take. Have you seen, or I should say, heard those? I guess the parents are so enamored by the fact that their precious little ones can walk that they want to hear every single step they make. They never take into consideration that everyone else in the room might not be quite so enamored with the squeak every other second.

Busy Calendars

Many times I have announced that we're going to start having an hour of reading time in our rooms every day, but then our days get so filled up running here and there that we never have time to enforce it. Such things were easier when our children were younger and we were at home more, but I'm going to go into full-confession mode. Here's a list of things I've said we were going to do that only lasted about one week or a month at best: every Thursday night dinner focusing on a different part of the world, learning another language together, twice-a-week family guitar lessons, daily devotional time, nightly family workout or dance party . . . you get the idea. Sometimes we have all of these great ideas, but then we fill up our calendars and never get around to doing them.

Part of our ability to be consistent as parents depends on our not having unrealistic expectations of ourselves. Perhaps, rather than saying that we're going to have a family dance party every night, we could say that we're going to do it once a week and keep flexible the scheduled night. Again, if you're a schedule-oriented person, you may be great at this—but for us, saying that we're going to do something on the same night every week is just setting ourselves up for failure.

Furthermore, we should take a hard look at our calendars to see what we can give up so that we'll have more time to do the important things and accomplish the goals we really want to accomplish as a family. Our calendars can get so filled up with kids' events that we don't realize that our children are running the show.

Sadie is our busy kid, even before *Duck Dynasty* and *Dancing with the Stars*. That's her personality. She always kept her social calendar handy, ready to schedule an invitation at a moment's notice. If she didn't have anything planned, she would ask me if we could have a party or invite a friend over to go to the mall. I had to help this child slow down a bit and realize there are six other people who live in our household. Whereas John Luke was totally content to stay home or go fishing or exploring in the yard in the summertime, Sadie had a list of five different camps she wanted to attend. I had to limit Sadie to two camps and had to force John Luke to pick two. Sadie's year would go straight from basketball to track to tennis to softball, and she even begged us to let her play football in seventh grade. I'm not kidding. She got her throwing arm from her Papaw Phil and could throw a football as well as any boy on the football team. The coach told her that if she could convince us to let her play, she would be the quarterback. The problem was, she only weighed about seventy pounds, and I was afraid she would get pummeled. We told her that if she broke something playing football, it would totally screw up basketball season, so she'd better just stick with her other sports.

I do want my kids to be busy and learn new things, but I don't want one child to run the family calendar. Part of growing up is learning that you don't get to do everything you want to, and it's probably not in your best interest anyway. Consistently sending this message will teach your child that living in a community means being considerate of everyone's schedule.

The Fear Factor

The last point I want to make about consistency may seem over the top, but I have seen this. For lots of reasons, some parents are afraid of their kids, and that fear keeps them from doing what they need to do. I'm sure you've seen such parents in the grocery store checkout line. The child asks for candy, the mom says no, the child begins what promises to be a full-blown fit, and the mom quickly hands over the candy so as not to be embarrassed by the brewing temper tantrum. I'm sure we've all been that parent at one time or another, but please don't give in to this kind of pressure. We've all been through the "terrible twos." Parents seem afraid to discipline the squalling toddler, so they handle him as if he's a time bomb waiting to explode. I understand their concern. Every parent of a toddler has experienced seeing their child go from smiling to screaming in five seconds flat. I know, it *is* scary. But the answer isn't tiptoeing around the child to keep him from exploding. Being scared of a child always leads to poor parenting decisions. Please don't give in to the temper tantrums just because other people are watching. Every parent of older children has been there, done that. Your child writhing on the floor of the supermarket is not a sign of bad parenting. It's a good sign that your child is in the process of learning that the world doesn't revolve around him, and sometimes that isn't pretty, but it has to happen sometime or another. If you don't teach this during the toddler stage, as your child grows older, the temper tantrums may look different, but they won't go away. They'll just take different forms, and I promise you they will be much more difficult and scary than walking out of the door of the grocery store with a crying toddler.

CHILDREN NEED CONSISTENCY

Studies show that inconsistency can make children feel insecure and confused. Think about the things that are consistent in your life—your job, your paycheck, your spouse. When those things stop being consistent, your world is rattled. As inconsistent as I admit that I am, when things like my job, our home life, or the way Willie treats me become inconsistent, I might feel insecure. Our kids are the same way. They depend on our consistency. They need to be able to know that certain things in their life will stay the same. Our kids need to be secure in the relationship that Willie and I have; they need to know that we will have food on the table and a roof over their heads; they need to know we will discipline them in a loving, consistent way, and that we will always love them unconditionally.

I realize that there are times, sadly, when big things happen to families: marriages fall apart, parents lose their jobs, families lose their homes, devastating illnesses strike. If your family is going through some upheaval right now, it's even more crucial to be consistent in the way you treat your children. The consistent way you love and discipline them will cover a multitude of inconsistencies in areas that you cannot control. I've watched some of our family members go through difficult marriages and divorces, but they have worked hard to keep consistent everything they could control. One of my good friends was a single mom for nearly ten years. She never excused herself from consistently loving and training her children, and she never excused her children's behavior. So when uncertainties or upheavals arose, such as issues over what time the children would spend with each parent, these children still had the security of knowing what their mom expected from them and what they could expect from their mom. These kids have grown into amazing young people who love God and both their parents.

Consistency is one of the many ways you communicate to your children that they are important to you. When the discipline is inconsistent, children never know what is expected of them in life, and that can be very confusing. Again, think of your job. How much would you respect a boss who is sometimes kind and understanding when you come to work fifteen minutes late but other times chews you out? Our kids feel the same way. Treating children inconsistently will cause them to lose respect for us, and it's not an effective way to help them learn. When children know what to expect, it helps them make informed decisions. As they grow, they learn that certain behaviors lead to certain outcomes.

TIPS FOR BEING CONSISTENT

No one is consistent 100 percent of the time. I get that we all do our best with each day and each child we're given. But being consistent should be a priority. When you mess up, stop and be honest with your kids. Tell them you were wrong to allow them to do what they did or to gripe at them about something minor just because you were in a bad mood; then start over. Here are a few things to remember in your quest for consistency.

Be Prepared for the Long Road

Training for anything doesn't happen overnight. If you've ever had a puppy, then you understand this completely. Synonyms of *consistent* are *steady, stable, even, regular,* and *uniform.* These are not words associated with a quick turnaround. Remember, giving in to children will bring quick results, but the potential exists for long-term problems. We have our children for eighteen years for a reason—it takes a while to grow them.

Circle the Wagons

When you're dealing with a child's particular problem area, it's time to circle the wagons. Get everyone on board to help. With our little challenger, Will, I had to be willing to let everyone know that he may need a little extra attention. It wouldn't have been in his best interest for me to act as if he didn't. While Willie and I were primarily responsible for molding and shaping him, it was in Will's best interest to let babysitters, grandparents, aunts and uncles, and teachers know that we knew his tricks and that he wasn't going to get them past us.

Your Kids May Not Like You

When you enforce discipline consistently, there will be times when your kids won't like you very much, and you have to be okay with that. I'm sure my kids have all taken turns thinking that I'm the meanest mom on the planet, but that's fine with me. Although I have a great relationship with each of our kids, my job has never been simply to be their friend. My job is to teach and train them to love God, each other, and their neighbors. Sometimes that job requires me to make some unpopular decisions. I promise you that they'll wake up the next morning and will still love you and think you're the best. I love that about a kid. They live one day at a time. We should all be so forgiving.

Don't Back Yourself in a Corner

I've done it. You probably have too. "If you say that one more time, you're not getting out of your room for the rest of the night."

Oh dear, it's out there, and you forgot that tonight is the big basketball game the family was going to together. Now what? The best way to handle that is not to get there in the first place. When a child disobeys, you don't have to give out the punishment immediately. In fact, some thinking time is good for a kid. Tell him you'll get back to him later, and let him stew about what the punishment might be. Then you have time to think through the options and make a wise decision that punishes the child involved and not the whole family. But if you find yourself in a situation like the example above, you can still get out of that corner. Just say, "I know I told you that you had to stay in tonight, but I don't want to punish the whole family for something you did. You will be allowed to go tonight, but your punishment will be cleaning the garage on Saturday."

Consistency. It says love, and it creates security. When I think of this word, I can't help but think of another area where consistency matters. If you watch the show at all, you know that I'm not the best cook. Over the years Miss Kay has tried to teach me. With many recipes she says, "Look at the consistency to see if you've mixed it right." Yes, even in cooking, consistency matters. When you get it right, as Miss Kay will tell you, you'll have a delicious piecrust—and some pretty great kids.

Willie's Words on Being Consistent

One of the biggest mistakes I see parents make is in not being consistent. I get it, sometimes after a long day of dealing with people out in the world, you just want to sit in your recliner and watch the golf channel. The last thing you want to do is get up to take whatever it is away from your child that you've told him not to pick up. The problem is kids know this. If I'm not consistent with my discipline as a dad, my kids will continue to test the limits. When they are young, this may mean pushing the button on the television that you've told them not to touch, but as they get older testing the limits has much greater consequences. Consequences that could affect them for their entire lives.

For some reason I remember more stories like this about John Luke and Will than about our girls. Maybe I was tougher on them because they were boys, or maybe they tested the limits more. It was probably a little of both. I remember both boys, if you said don't cross that line, would get as close to the line as possible and watch to see if you weren't paying attention and then stick a toe across it. Since you're reading this, I'm assuming you have kids and know exactly what I'm talking about. It was important that I was there to discipline them every time they crossed that line, not just when I felt like it.

I was not the kind of dad who counted to three. When I asked our kids to do something, I meant it, and I meant it to happen right then. I always had a visual in my mind of my telling one of our children to stop, but the child didn't obey and ran into oncoming traffic. That vision motivated me to teach them that when I said, "Stop," I meant it. The only way to teach your kids to obey when you say it the first time is through consistently following through with discipline when they don't obey. Many people have commented on how polite, respectful, and obedient our kids are. It's true, they are great kids who honor us as parents. Consistency in parenting is not easy, but trust me, it's worth it.

EIGHTEEN

BE LOVING

So much has been written about love. Maybe you've heard that the English language is one of the few that doesn't have different words to describe the different ways we love. We say that we *love* ice cream and we *love* our grandparents. However, we know what we mean by both of these phrases. Our feelings for ice cream are so weak compared to the feelings we have for our grandparents, yet we use the same word—*love*.

The Bible describes the importance of love like this:

> If I could speak all the languages of earth and of angels, but didn't love others, I would only be a noisy gong or a clanging cymbal. If I had the gift of prophecy, and if I understood all of God's secret plans and possessed all knowledge, and if I had such faith that I could move mountains, but didn't love others, I would be nothing. If I gave everything I have to the poor and even sacrificed my body, I could boast about it; but if I didn't love others, I would have gained nothing. (1 Cor. 13:1–3 NLT)

And then there's God's love. That's the love we are challenged to emulate. But what does that kind of love look like when we show it to our kids?

GOD'S LOVE FOR US

I've read several books from people who have had near-death experiences. I don't think it's a coincidence that every account I've ever read has essentially the same message. Each person talks about a feeling of immense love that he or she cannot adequately describe.

Our heavenly Father loves us in a way that is beyond words. The apostle Paul wrote about God's love for us like this: "I pray that you, being rooted and established in love, may have power, together with all the Lord's holy people, to grasp how wide and long and high and deep is the love of Christ, and to know this love that surpasses knowledge —that you may be filled to the measure of all the fullness of God" (Eph. 3:17–19).

These verses almost dare us to try to understand God's love for us. Paul uses these four words: *wide, long, high,* and *deep.* These are simple measurements we can all understand because we think in finite terms. Paul, in his humanity, knew that we, in our humanity, couldn't possibly understand a love that surpasses knowledge, a love that is infinite. Words like *wide, long, high,* and *deep* only serve to get us a few steps closer to understanding God's love for us, which is beyond anything we can ever imagine.

However, if we just pay attention, we do feel and see glimpses of God's great love. Think of the peaceful feeling you get when you see a sunset brilliantly painted in shades of purple and red, the joy you feel when your toes are curled in the sand and a tiny wave washes over them, or the comfort you feel when you smell a fire warming your hearth on a cold winter day. Even if you've never experienced any of those events, close your eyes and imagine them. Now, think how much the God who gives His children such magnificent gifts must love us.

I think that we're never closer to understanding the love our heavenly Father has for us than when we see our children for the first time. What a gift a baby is! With our large family we are never lacking a baby to hold. To see what magic God applies to each child as He forms a new creation from two loving parents is truly breathtaking. I'll never forget the joy I felt when our firstborn, John Luke, wiggled his little mouth and I saw that he had a dimple just like his daddy's.

Yes, the love we have for our own perfect baby is the love God has for us. That's because He looks at us new every morning. Lamentations

3:22–23 says, "Because of the Lord's great love we are not consumed, / for his compassions never fail. / They are new every morning; / great is your faithfulness." As humans we get bogged down in everyday life. We have a hard time moving beyond past hurts and troubles. But just as we see newborns with plenty of hope and promise for tomorrow and no past failures to temper our love for them, that's how God sees and loves us. What happened yesterday or the minute before is gone and will be remembered no more. If we could love like that, the world would be a much better place.

On this earth, though, we *are* flawed. We have been hurt by sin and tragedy; we have feelings of guilt and shame, and sometimes those things inhibit our ability to feel loved and to be loving toward others in turn. The sooner we recognize the problems that guilt and shame bring to our lives, the sooner we can move toward resolving them. My prayer is that, if you have trouble moving on from hurts of the past, you will spend time praying, reading, and meditating on God's Word, or talking to a friend or counselor so you can move past your hurts and get closer to knowing and giving the kind of love God is offering to you.

Showing Love to Our Children

Having a feeling of love for our children—or anyone else—is one thing, but showing it is another. How do we put love into action? How do we act lovingly even when we don't feel loving? We all know that, after a while, being the mom of a child who has more energy than the Energizer Bunny, who will argue with a stop sign, and who loves to appear in your bedroom at 3:30 a.m., takes a toll on even the best relationships. We love our children, but sometimes liking them is not so easy.

I feel very fortunate to have grown up in a home that was full of love. My parents love each other and loved us children—I knew it. They didn't just tell me they loved me; their actions showed they loved me. Because of their example, I understand what it means to be loved and how to be loving. Being a loving mother doesn't mean that I act like a Disney princess every day. Now, I love Disney princesses as much as the next person does, and I know some women who seem to have that personality naturally, but that's not me. It's not most people. For most of us, life is not all sunshine and roses. We get tired, frustrated, or in a funk and act in ways that aren't very princesslike. That's part of being real. Being loving doesn't mean that you have to always have a smile on your face and talk in a soft, high-pitched voice. What it does mean is that your home should feel like a loving place, a place where your children, spouse, friends, and family want to be. It means that when we come out of that funk and realize that we haven't been the most pleasant person to be around, we apologize and move on. It means that your family should know, beyond a shadow of a doubt, that they are loved unconditionally by their heavenly Father, God, and by their parents without reservation and to the moon and back.

Love in Action

Have you ever been through the process of building or remodeling a house? Counselors say that it's really tough on a marriage. Stressors include the house plans themselves; how much money should be spent; frustrations with the builder, painter, and plumber; and adding another job to your already busy lives—it can be stressful! Willie and I have built a few houses during our married life. It hasn't been that big of a stressor for us, mainly because I really like the process and Willie pretty much stays out of it—except for the kitchen, where he makes sure he has a good gas stove with a griddle, a giant refrigerator, a freezer for all of his deer meat, and, in the den, a good-sized television that is approximately ten feet from his comfy recliner. (I guess I should add the remote too!) Trust me, there are other things we argue and disagree about, but building a house isn't one of them.

When I was in middle school, my family built a new home. I don't remember what prompted the argument, and my parents probably don't either, but I remember their extreme stress when the argument broke out. I remember crying on the couch one day (middle school is an emotional and dramatic time for everyone, right?), worried that they were fighting too much and were going to end up getting a divorce. My mom saw me, and I told her what was wrong. She hugged and kissed me and assured me that they would never divorce. She assured me that she and Daddy loved each other; they were simply disagreeing and would be more careful to disagree more lovingly so that I didn't worry. My fears were alleviated. Our new home was soon completed, and all was well.

This was a good lesson for me in a couple of ways. First, we will go through times in our marriages when we disagree, but it doesn't mean that we don't love each other. Second, our kids are attuned to our relationships; when we don't act lovingly toward our spouses, they can feel insecure. Since disagreements are inevitable, we must strive to keep them to a minimum while staying as loving as possible. How we treat others is love in action. Our children might cover their eyes and groan when we kiss and hug in front of them, but it reassures them that we love each other. The little things—hugging and kissing, bragging about each other, putting love letters on each other's mirrors, fixing their favorite meal (Willie's good at this one!), or just holding each other's hands—show our children love in action.

The word *love* is in the Bible more than five hundred times. God takes love and the expression of love seriously. In Matthew 22:37–39, Jesus said, "'Love the Lord your God with all your heart and with all your soul and with all your mind.' This is the first and greatest commandment. And the second is like it: 'Love your neighbor as yourself.'"

LOVE OUR NEIGHBORS

How are we to love our neighbors? We should love our neighbors in the same way we love ourselves. Fortunately the Bible has a lot of really good examples of love, and one amazing definition is found in 1 Corinthians 13:4–8.

Love is patient, love is kind. It does not envy, it does not boast, it is not proud. It does not dishonor others, it is not self-seeking, it is not easily angered, it keeps no record of wrongs. Love does not delight in evil but rejoices with the truth. It always protects, always trusts, always hopes, always perseveres.

Love never fails.

When I was a teenager, our youth minister had us write out this passage, replacing the word *love* with our names. So for me, it read, "Korie is patient, Korie is kind. Korie does not envy, she does not boast, she is not proud. Korie does not dishonor others, she is not self-seeking, she is not easily angered, she keeps no record of wrongs. Korie does not delight in evil but rejoices with the truth. She always protects, always trusts, always hopes, always perseveres. Korie never fails."

Wow, that's pretty powerful, right? Do this right now for yourself. It will challenge you in profound ways. Repeat this to yourself when you wake up in the morning and, I promise you, your day will be different—not because everyone around you will be different, but because *you* will be, and how you react to those around you will be different. It will truly change your life.

The Father's Love for Us

The story of the prodigal son, found in Luke 15:11–24, is another beautiful example of love in the Bible.

There was a man who had two sons. The younger one said to his father, "Father, give me my share of the estate." So he divided his property between them.

Not long after that, the younger son got together all he had, set off for a distant country and there squandered his wealth in wild living. After he had spent everything, there was a severe famine in that whole country, and he began to be in need. So he went and hired himself out to a citizen of that country, who sent him to his fields to feed pigs. He longed to fill his stomach with the pods that the pigs were eating, but no one gave him anything.

When he came to his senses, he said, "How many of my father's hired servants have food to spare, and here I am starving to death! I will set out and go back to my father and say to him: Father, I have sinned against heaven and against you. I am no longer worthy to be called your son; make me like one of your hired servants." So he got up and went to his father.

But while he was still a long way off, his father saw him and was filled with compassion for him; he ran to his son, threw his arms around him and kissed him.

The son said to him, "Father, I have sinned against heaven and against you. I am no longer worthy to be called your son."

But the father said to his servants, "Quick! Bring the best robe and put it on him. Put a ring on his finger and sandals on his feet. Bring the fattened calf and kill it. Let's have a feast and celebrate. For this son of mine was dead and is alive again; he was lost and is found."

The message of this parable is so redeeming. A child who has lost his way is welcomed back into the arms of a loving parent. The dad didn't argue with or try to shame the son to keep him from making such a big mistake. Rather, he let him go to learn his own lessons.

The father undoubtedly knew that the son's course was a risky one. I'm sure that the father wasn't happy about his son's decision. One can almost imagine a mom in the background saying, "Are you seriously going to let him go?" The father allowed his son to go into the world to face the troubles and trials of the world—alone. And when the son finally realized that he'd made a mistake, his father welcomed him home with open arms. That's the kind of love God has for us too.

Love Children Enough to Discipline Them

Another aspect of love that the Bible teaches is discipline. We should love our children enough to discipline them. Hebrews 12:5–11 says:

Have you completely forgotten this word of encouragement that addresses you as a father addresses his son? It says,

"My son, do not make light of the Lord's discipline,
and do not lose heart when he rebukes you,
because the Lord disciplines the one he loves,
and he chastens everyone he accepts as his son."

Endure hardship as discipline; God is treating you as his children. For what children are not disciplined by their father? If you are not disciplined—and everyone undergoes discipline—then you are not legitimate, not true sons and daughters at all. Moreover, we have all had human fathers who disciplined us and we respected them for it. How much more should we submit to the Father of spirits and live! They disciplined us for a little while as they thought best; but God disciplines us for our good, in order that we may share in his holiness. No discipline seems pleasant at the time, but painful. Later on, however, it produces a harvest of righteousness and peace for those who have been trained by it.

And Proverbs 13:24 says, "Those who spare the rod of discipline hate their children. / Those who love their children care enough to discipline them" (NLT).

The word *discipline* has gotten a bad rap because we tend to equate discipline with punishment. Discipline does sometimes imply punishment, but more than that, discipline is about training. Parents who love their children will lovingly discipline them, knowing that it's the right way to lead them to adulthood. The Hebrews passage underscores that a lack of discipline shows a lack of love. Remember, discipline is evidence of love, not the absence of it.

We let our children know that if we didn't love them, we would let them act any way they wanted to; we wouldn't care what they did. But because we love them, it is our job to discipline them and help them become the kind of people God wants them to be. From child development studies we know that children left on their own will do what anyone left on his or her own would do. Throughout their lives they will make poor decisions and mistakes with money, will struggle with relationship issues, and will have trouble reaching goals. Children who have not been taught to listen to instruction, obey those in authority, respect those around them, and be alert to the laws of the land are headed for lifelong troubles.

Our children should have a healthy respect for and fear of us when they are young, just as God demands a healthy respect and fear for Him. The Bible talks a lot about the fact that we should fear God. This seems incompatible with the love we've talked about, but when we are immature in our faith, as when children are young, fear instills healthy motivation to do what's right. Obeying out of fear gives way, ultimately, to doing what is right because we love God and trust that He only asks of us what is best for us. It will be the same way for our children with us. When they are young, we must let them know that they are loved completely and that we love them enough to discipline them. If we do our jobs right as parents, as they mature, they'll see that our motives were love and the desire to see them become happy and healthy adults.

My mom used to say to us, "I love you too much to let you continue to act that way." This was a powerful message, and it's one we pass on to our kids. She let us know that she was disciplining us not because she was mad at us or because she thought we were bad kids but because she loved us and wanted what was best for us. This is how God loves us and how we should love our children.

The topic of love is so huge, I am barely making a dent! I've been blessed to be surrounded by love from my physical family as well as my church family. But I'm sad to acknowledge that this isn't true for everyone. Yet I know this: God loves you and me with a love that is hard to describe and difficult to understand. On your darkest of days, remember the reassuring truth from John 3:16: "God so loved the world that he gave his one and only Son, that whoever believes in him shall not perish but have eternal life."

Willie's Words on Being Loving

Being strong and confident, especially as a dad, does not mean that we should love less or not be soft and tender with our children. Those moments should be more frequent than the stronger moments required for disobedience. But it takes both strong love and strong discipline to create a healthy environment for children. My goal as a dad is that my children will know that I'll always love them and take care of them but that I will also be strong enough to discipline them. It can be a tricky balance, but if your heart is right, you can make it happen.

I'm so blessed that my mom and dad loved us enough to share their faith with us. Because of Dad's decision to live for Jesus, we were exposed to many life lessons on love.

One of my favorite stories of love is about a sweet woman at our church. I had graduated from high school and started attending a seminary that was held at our local church. A few families had committed to giving twenty-five dollars a month to help with books and stuff, but I was basically broke. I was in the lobby of church one day when Miss Willa came up and handed me a ten-dollar bill. I knew she didn't have much money because she had kids and grandkids she was helping out and no husband to help her. Her job was cleaning the church building, which didn't pay her much. And here she was showing a young kid like me what truly loving and caring for someone means. To this day I'm surprised I even took the money, but then again I think it's important to accept people's gifts of love. A big part of love is being able to receive love from others.

We all know that actions speak louder than words. We have no greater example of love than the one of Jesus' ultimate sacrifice for us. I want my children to know that love from their heavenly Father and from me, their earthly father.

NINETEEN

BE TRUTHFUL

In our family we talk about everything—and I mean everything. From a young age, our children have heard stories of their Papaw Phil and Mamaw Kay's difficult years as well as tough times in the marriages of their aunts and uncles and in Willie's and mine. We talk about the struggles, about God's love for us through them all, and about how He brought us through the storms and to the other side.

We covered the value of instilling the character trait of honesty in our children in an earlier chapter. This chapter about being truthful is more about how we, as parents, present ourselves to our children in a real and truthful way.

When I was growing up, my family talked about a lot of things, but not to the extent that the Robertson family did. I'll admit, at first it was a little embarrassing. When Willie and I were dating, I had to be prepared for Phil to ask us about our relationship or give advice on how to make sure that Willie was "keeping it in his pants." Yes, that's a direct quote from Phil on how to avoid sex before marriage. The Robertsons are straight shooters; they don't really censor themselves for the kids who might be in the room. It's all out there, and I've come to love this about our family. Not talking about something doesn't make it go away. And because we talk with our kids about anything and everything, perhaps they'll feel comfortable coming to us in the hard times of life instead of to a friend or boyfriend who may not be doling out the best advice.

ANSWER KIDS' QUESTIONS TRUTHFULLY

Willie and I talk a lot to our kids, and we try to answer every question as openly and truthfully as we can. We still laugh at the memory of telling each of our kids how babies are made because each one's reaction was so different. Sex is something good that God made, and we wanted our kids to get that message from us instead of the message that it's something scary that's not to be talked about. We certainly didn't want them learning about sex from someone else. When our children were young, we decided that when the time came, we were just going to answer the question as openly and truthfully as possible, making it age-appropriate, of course.

So one day, when she was somewhere around fourth grade, Sadie asked me a question, and I felt she was old enough to really understand. We were watching TV, and someone said something about a woman being "sexy." "What does *sexy* mean?" Sadie asked me. She and I were alone, so I thought, *Now's the time; I might as well go ahead and tell her.* I explained to her that the word *sexy* comes from the word *sex,* and then went on to explain what sex is. Now most kids get really quiet when you tell them about sex. At least that's what happened with each of our other children. It's always a little bit of an uncomfortable situation for everyone involved, so looking at the ground and staying quiet seems to fit the occasion. Not for Sadie. She started dying laughing and literally fell off the couch laughing so hard.

When she finally finished laughing, I asked, "What is so funny?"

She said, "Never in a million years would I have thought of that!" We laughed some more at that! Then she went on to ask me every question you could possibly imagine about sex, and I mean everything. We talked for a couple of hours with me trying to answer openly and truthfully, just as I'd planned.

At the end of it, she said, "I'm not sure I wanted to know all of that."

I said, "Baby, I'm your mama, and whatever you ask me, I'm always going to answer you openly and truthfully because I want you to know that there's absolutely nothing that we can't talk about."

We want our children to talk to us, right? We want them to come to us with their successes and their failures. If we dodge their questions, if we portray ourselves as perfect, and if we change the subject when things come up that are messy or uncomfortable, we won't have the relationship that we want to have with our kids. We won't have the benefit of being the ones to sow good seeds into them, to give them advice when they need it. We won't have the privilege of being the shoulder they cry on when a boyfriend breaks up with them, when a friend lets them down, or when they mess up and do something they know will disappoint you. They'll go instead to the friend who will listen without judging, but that friend may not be able to truly help or be a good example or influence them for good. Even worse, they may clam up, lock themselves in their rooms, and try to deal with all those tough teenage emotions alone.

Be an Example of Truthfulness

Don't overlook the importance of your own example of truthfulness. It's essential that our kids see us being truthful with our spouse, in our business dealings, and with our friends. Children pick up on the little things. When you are dishonest about the little things, what's to keep you from being dishonest about the big ones? "Do as I say and not as I do" doesn't work when teaching truthfulness or any other positive value. Our kids will do what they see us doing, and if we aren't truthful with them or in front of them, they won't be truthful with us, and they will learn not to trust us or others.

Another way we as parents have to model truthfulness is by saying what we mean and meaning what we say. I'm talking about staying true to our word. The Bible says, "Let your 'Yes' be 'Yes,' and your 'No,' 'No'" (Matt. 5:37 NKJV). This is a tough one because our kids ask a thousand things of us every day, and we give quick answers that we sometimes regret later. This is one that I've had to learn over the years and admit I'm not always very good at it. Our kids can tell when I'm distracted. They might ask me if they can go somewhere or do something that I might have said no to if they asked me at a less-distracted moment. Later they'll say, "Remember, Mom, you said I could do that." But I don't remember! So I try to be really careful about what I agree to and let my yes be yes. I'm just as careful with what I say no to. Sometimes we parents say no just because we're in a bad mood; then we realize later that maybe it was something we could have said yes to in the first place. Then we find ourselves in a conundrum.

By this time the child has usually begged, whined, and complained . . . so now we don't want to say yes because then said child thinks he got what he wanted because he whined. So now, even though we don't mind if the child gets what he wants or goes to the party after all, at this point, we have to allow our "no" to be "no." Such is parenting! So back to being truthful with your kids—go ahead and throw out a "let me think about it" every once in a while, and this principle will be much easier to live out.

Be Careful with Your Praise

Finally is the issue of how we communicate to our kids about their strengths, abilities, and weaknesses. We've all done it: we clapped at their first steps and applauded when they mastered counting from one to ten. Of course we did! We love it when our children figure out a new skill, but then we must move on. I'm not saying that giving our children encouragement is wrong, but as a society we climbed on the praise train about the same time the self-esteem train was boarding. We were told that praising our children would give them confidence so they'd face the world with an I-can-do-it attitude (thank you, Bob the Builder). But somewhere in all that positive thinking, we forgot to see whether the theory works. Now, many years into heaping praise on our little ones, it seems that research isn't backing up the theory. In fact, research has shown that too much praise is detrimental to children. Goodness! It's like experts telling us that coffee is bad for us, then it was good, and now it's bad. Someone, please decide! Well, I'm going to keep drinking my coffee, but the research on praise seems pretty convincing. We need to dial it down.

First, evidence shows that children get addicted to praise. This really doesn't require a ten-year study. I've seen it myself. If we praise our children for every action they take, they'll begin to need our praise to continue the task. The danger here is that someday at school or work, no one will praise them, and they'll think that they've done something wrong. Our children must learn to do tasks because it's the right thing to do, not because someone will sit beside them and tell them, "Good job!"

Another important finding is that children who are praised often lose motivation and resiliency. Carol Dweck, a researcher from Stanford University who studies children's coping skills, studied children who were fourteen to thirty-eight months old. (That's the age when parents clap the most.) Her research showed that, as they grew older, children who had been praised for the process ("you tried really hard") were more resilient and eager to learn than were those who were praised for who they are ("you're really smart"). She concluded that praising children for their intelligence or abilities often undermines motivation and hurts performance.[1] It seems that kids who are told they are smart care more about their performance goals and less about learning while kids praised for their efforts believe that trying hard really matters.

If we tell our kids that they're great at everything, are overly complimentary, and gush over them at every turn, then they won't believe us even when we're giving them praise that is truly warranted. We've all been around parents who go overboard with this. Every time the child poops, it is deemed to be the greatest poop that ever came out of a child. We all do this to some extent as new parents. Willie jokes with me and says that I think every child is brilliant. It's kind of true; I love children, and I love to see how their little minds work. They crack me up and delight me. But there comes a point when we can go overboard with this.

We've all seen the dad on the sidelines praising and bragging on his kid every time he takes a step. Cut to the kid rolling his eyes at every

"Great job" his dad utters. Children know what's praiseworthy and what isn't, and if we constantly praise our kids for meaningless, simple accomplishments, they won't feel rewarded when they've truly worked hard and have done a task well. Even worse, they might not even try.

We used to love to watch *American Idol*, but it always amazed me when parents of some of the teenagers would go on and on about what amazing singers their children are. Then, when the children got their chance in front of the judges, they clearly were not amazing. In fact, many times they were horrible! I've often wondered, *Can they truly not hear it?* Or had their overzealous encouragement gotten so out of hand that when their children announced they were trying out for *American Idol*, they had to let them do it or admit that they'd been lying all along?

My parents brought me up to believe I could do or be anything I wanted in life; I simply needed to learn it and work hard at it. I think this has served me well. This is how Willie and I have tried to raise our children as well. He has told me many times that this is something I brought to the table in our marriage; the confidence I had in him—and in us—to accomplish whatever dream we decided to pursue helped him believe in himself and believe that he could actually grow Duck Commander to where it is today, have a hit television show, and keep up with all the other crazy things going on in our lives right now. I never really doubted it. I do see the best in people and try to praise their strengths rather than look at their weaknesses. I was raised to believe that "'with God all things are possible'" (Matt. 19:26), and I truly believe that.

Having said that, this type of communication is very different from telling your children they're the next Michelangelo when they draw their first scribble on paper. At some point your kids will realize that you weren't telling them the truth—or they won't, and then they'll struggle to find a job that isn't "beneath" them. They'll have a hard time listening to their coaches, and they'll struggle with relationships when the other person points out their obvious flaws.

While raising me to believe that I could do or be anything I wanted in life, my parents also taught me to be realistic about my strengths and weaknesses. For instance, I knew that I wasn't the most athletic in the family, but that didn't mean I didn't play and work hard at sports. I was tall and skinny, and it took me a while to grow into my body type. Trust me, running down the basketball court or throwing a softball was a little awkward. Because my parents were truthful with me about what I was good at and what I needed to work a little harder at, I was able to laugh at myself and keep on playing—even that time when I was running backward to catch a ball and practically did a back flip. Yes, that did happen.

I read a great article the other day that featured this sentence: "You're talented, but talent is overrated."[2] There's a book stating this same premise written by Geoff Colvin.[3] Both the article writer and Mr. Colvin make some excellent points. Willie and I have always encouraged and built up our children, but we also try to help our kids learn to laugh at themselves for the things they're not so good at. For instance, in our family we have three good singers (Willie, Sadie, and Will), three not-so-good singers, and one (Rebecca) who is somewhere in the middle. John Luke, Bella, and I are the not-so-good singers; it's something we all fully acknowledge, laugh about, and ultimately embrace. One day, just the three of us happened to be in the car, and Bella said, "Hey, none of the good singers are with us; we can belt it out without worrying about them laughing at us." So we turned the music up and laughed and sang at the top of our lungs. We may not be the best, but we don't care; we sing anyway and can have fun doing it!

Will is our best singer. He's always had perfect pitch, always been on the beat, and could even harmonize from a pretty young age, so he's the one most bothered by our bad singing. One day he said to Bella, "Bella, you're way off the note."

Bella replied, "Have you ever thought that I wanted to sing it like that?" You go, girl! Bella let Will know that she might not be hitting the note the singer was on, but maybe that's exactly the way she wanted to sing it. This makes me laugh just to think of it! Having confidence in who you are is not believing you're the best at everything; it's about being secure in who you are and knowing that while you may not be the best at everything, you can be the best *you* that you can be.

I'm so glad that all of my children have different personalities, gifts, and talents. While it's certainly challenging for us parents, it makes life so much more exciting to have different personalities living under the same roof, not to mention that it's a great training ground to prepare kids for getting out into the real world, which is filled with many different personalities. In our family Rebecca is artsy and funny, and she knows what she wants; John Luke loves to learn new things, reads nearly a book a day, and is always ready for an adventure; Sadie is outgoing, athletic, and empathetic toward others; Will loves to meet new people, always remembers a face and a name, and is very musical; Bella is a fun story-teller, is thoughtful of others, and is great with dates and numbers—she is the one who will remember your birthday or anniversary.

I'm sure your family is just as varied. While this is a partial list of who our kids are and what their strengths are, it doesn't tell you every-thing about them. Be careful not to put your kids in a box and make them feel trapped in a certain fixed identity. Believe in them, tell them they can do anything they want to in life, but don't be that mom or dad who is always over their shoulder yelling, "That's awesome! You're the best!" Teach them to laugh about the things they're not good at, or, if it's something they really want to be good at, encourage them to work at it. The same is true for you. Take a class; go back to school; do the things it takes to be really good at whatever you want to be good at. If you've told your children that they're the best at everything, they won't put in the time and hard work it takes to be really great.

TRADE WORDS FOR ACTIONS

So what's a reformed praise parent to do? This really boils down to simply trading your words for actions. Let's use the example of your child's learning to tie his shoes. That's a difficult task and one for which you certainly would want to praise your child once he has mastered it. Using words like, "You did it! You tied your shoes all by yourself! Good job!" acknowledges the difficulty of the task and applauds your child's hard work. This tells him hard work brings results. If you say, "You're so smart! I'm proud of how smart you are," you're applauding something over which he has no control—intelligence. Resolve to praise your children's hard work and effort, not their God-given ability.

Many parents want to know how they can praise one child's talent when the other child doesn't have the same talent. The answer is to praise the good efforts of all of them equally and acknowledge that facts are facts. Will is very musical; John Luke is not. But for Will to succeed in music, he still must work hard. Just ask someone on the top of the talent pool, like Carrie Underwood. She still practices for many hours before any performance or recording. When we praise talent alone, we ignore an important component—effort.

Everyone is talented in some way, but not all talents are equally valued by the world. Athletics, music, and art are three of the most visible areas of talent our children can have, and the world highly values these talents. Few children will be talented in all of those areas; some won't be talented in any of them. Since we have a big family and live close to each other, it's important for us to acknowledge the strengths of each family member.

One way we work to avoid any comparison or jealousy that may creep in is by remembering that God has a plan for everyone's life, and He gives everyone exactly what they need to fulfill His plan, not ours. What we do is not about us. It's ultimately about giving glory and honor to God, and there are lots of ways we can do that.

Don't be afraid to be truthful with your children about their talents. Being truthful and realistic will take them further than will letting them believe something that isn't true (flashback to *American Idol*). If your child loves to sing but can't carry a tune in a bucket, tell her that you love that she loves to sing, but don't tell her she's the next Beyoncé. Have simple discussions about talents, reminding your child that everyone has different talents and that it takes all kinds to make a world. Don't make it into a big deal. It's life.

Like you, I want my children to feel encouraged and empowered to be whoever they want to be. But I also want them to be able to take criticism, to work hard, and to be realistic about their abilities. I want them to know that I love them because they're my children and that they don't need to do anything else for me to love them more. If they can truly understand this concept from their relationship with me, then they'll transfer that knowledge to their relationship with God.

TRUTHFULNESS IS LIKE A KISS

Okay, so maybe I got off on a few tangents in this chapter about truthfulness, but I hope you can see that if we talk to our children and answer their tough questions, if we teach them to tell the truth in their relationships, and if we are realistic and truthful with them in our praise and encouragement, we will help produce children of good character.

Proverbs 24:26 says, "An honest answer / is like a kiss on the lips." How sweet is that thought? A kiss suggests an intimate, warm relationship. One to be trusted. We all value a relationship that can be trusted. Children need and cherish parents who are willing to lead them with open and truth-filled hearts to be truthful and open adults.

Willie's Words on Being Truthful

The Robertsons value truthfulness. Korie has told you how we will pretty much say anything, especially if we think it will get a laugh. But that's just one kind of truthfulness. When I think back to my being a kid, I remember Mom and Dad really struggled to pay bills. We didn't have a lot of material things or nice clothes and toys. But when we sat around the dinner table at night, we knew our parents enjoyed each other and valued putting in a hard day's work.

At one point my mom had gone to work for a really good

man. That man, Mr. Brasher, took an interest in Dad's duck call ideas and decided to invest in him. That was probably my first impression of an honest businessman who wanted to help out another honest man. He loaned my dad twenty-five thousand dollars, and that was the beginning of Duck Commander.

I want our children to understand that hard work and honesty are truly the keys to a successful life. In our business today, I depend on honest employees. It would be heartbreaking if one of my own children weren't as honest as an employee. I want my children to be men and women who can be trusted. That's not to say we haven't dealt with our kids' not telling us the truth. We have. But we've handled it as quickly as it happened.

I also want them to understand the importance of truthfulness in a relationship. Korie and I let our kids know we trust each other by supporting each other in business decisions, parenting decisions, and social activities. That doesn't mean we always agree on every issue. I've been to a few chick flicks, and she's been hunting. It just means we support each other.

My advice here is the same as it is in the other chapters: start when they're young. Talk about being truthful, and show them examples of truth-telling people. Brag on them when they tell the truth about something that happened. Help them understand that telling the truth is the better way to live. I think many times parents just don't talk about it. They expect their kids to just *get it*, but it might not happen if you depend on that method. Teach them how to be honest, and let them see you being truthful. That's how they will get it.

TWENTY

BE REAL

It seems that society today is clamoring for something real. *Organic* and *all natural* are buzzwords for everything from food to clothing to body lotion. Could it be that we're finally done with fake? I doubt it. Along with all the talk of going back to a more natural approach to living, our magazines and television screens are full of ads for products that include fake eyelashes, fake nails, fake tans, fake food, fake hair, and fake fur. There's still plenty of fake to go around.

But fake things don't last—well, except for Twinkies and Spam. Those have been around forever. Eventually, the fake tan fades and the eyelashes fall off. Fortunately, we're usually at home when that happens, which is the best place to get rid of fake anything. In the interest of full disclosure, when you're in the entertainment business, there are times for fake hair, false eyelashes, and a spray tan. It's fun to feel glam for one night or for a photo shoot, but it feels even better to get home and take it all off. Home is where we can be ourselves, take off our makeup, put on our stretchy pants, and just be. But being real in our homes can be more complex than just being free to walk around in a pair of sweatpants and our husband's T-shirt.

What exactly does it mean to be real? Here are several questions I want to explore as we talk about being real in our homes and as parents:

- Do we try to appear one way to the world while acting differently at home?
- Is the life we're living true to how God made us?

- Are we allowing our kids to see that being real can sometimes be messy?

Do You Act Differently in Public than at Home?

Let's discuss the first question. Kids are damaged when the inside of the family home doesn't match the outside impression. I'm talking about parents who put on a front to appear one way to everyone around them but then come home where they're totally different people. Nobody likes a hypocrite, yet I think that's exactly what our children see and think of us sometimes. They may not know the term or how to articulate it, but they see it, and it will affect them negatively. It will impact the level of respect they have for adults and how they approach and interact with the world as they grow up.

A very common reason people give for leaving the church is they're convinced it's full of hypocrites. A hypocrite is a person who pretends to have virtues, moral or religious beliefs, or principles that he or she does not actually possess, especially a person whose actions contradict stated beliefs. A perfect example is a person bragging about her humility. Hypocrites are deceivers and pretenders, so they may put on a false show of humility so that others will notice and commend them.

Are we doing that in our homes? Are we pretending that values such as honesty, kindness, patience, goodness, and self-control are important to us while living lives at home that demonstrate the opposite? Are you doing that? We do this when we gossip—we may be kind to others when face-to-face with them but belittle them behind closed doors. We do this when we lie about little things, perhaps saying, "Tell them I'm not home," when someone calls. We do it when we tell our kids not to tell their daddy how much money we spent at the mall. Yes, it's a problem when we appear to be one way in public and another way at home. It's also a problem when we burnish our appearance as the perfect little family when we're out in public but spend our time yelling and fighting behind closed doors.

Don't get me wrong. We've all had those moments when we've argued and griped right up until the time we walked through the doors of the church building, then quickly changed our tone and thrown a smile on our faces. If moments like that are just moments, there's no need to worry. Nobody's perfect. But when moments like that define your family, it's time to take a good look and make the changes necessary to really become the family you want others to think you are.

Have you seen the apps that can Photoshop or adjust your pictures to perfection? In seconds your skin can be flawless, your teeth glowing white, and any stray hairs smoothed into shape. While it's natural to want to put your best face forward, it's never good to present yourself as something you're not. Our family is often asked to do photo shoots, and when I am asked to choose, of course I always want to pick the best version of me. However, I don't ever want to pick a "fake" me, or a picture that has been doctored so much that it doesn't look like the real me.

Why do we work so hard to show others our best selves? Why do we give our best selves to the ones who matter to us the least? Then when we get home to the people we love the most and who love us the most, we offer them our worst—our gripy, unloving, selfish selves. I truly believe that being inconsistent with who you are, being one way at home and presenting yourself to the world as something else, is one of the most destructive things you can do as a parent. When we do this, we're asking our children to live a lie. Kids learn values by watching our actions, and this type of hypocrisy confuses them and diminishes their respect for us. You may not see this affecting your children when they are young, but during their teenage years, you'll definitely see the damage.

What I'm talking about in this chapter, being real, is not about whether you stay in your pajamas all day and then dress up to go out with friends. It's about your value system and the way you treat others. Certainly, we must act differently in the workplace or for a dinner out than we do at home. No one expects you to act exactly the same way at a board meeting as you would playing UNO with the kids. That would be silly. How we behave is one thing; what motivates that behavior is another. Whether our actions show the values by which we claim to live is the key here.

I've learned a few things in my twenty years of parenting—one is to never expect your children to do what you won't do. Willie and I know that if we want our children to view our value system as real and something important to live by, our own actions have to match our values. That means we don't try to get Lil' Will into a movie at the price of a twelve-year-old when he's really thirteen. (He looks like a fifteen-year-old, so that probably wouldn't work anyway. If you haven't seen him lately, he's a big boy.) That means we don't say things like, "You're short; no one will know you're too old for that ride."

This next one is huge today. I haven't allowed our kids to get a Facebook account until they're thirteen because that's the policy. To get one earlier, they'd have to lie about their age when setting up the account. It's just something we're not okay with them doing. At the time of this writing, Bella is only twelve, and she has joked that by the time she gets to join Facebook, it'll be only her and her great-aunt still on there. It also means that our children don't hear us looking for ways to cheat the government or the local grocery store or to avoid the aunt trying to get in touch with us.

Leading by example is the number one way to teach children any behavior you want them to have. Kids respond better to "Do as I do" than to "Do as I say." Jesus came to this earth not only to offer Himself as a sacrifice but also to be our example of how to live. God knew that His children need an example, a pattern, to follow. Our children need one too.

Some of my favorite memories are of hearing my children "do as we do" with each other when I was in the other room. I loved to hear our older children saying to the younger ones things like, "Great job, Sadie. You did really good coloring that page!" "Bella, you ate everything on your plate. You're going to grow up big and strong." "Will, that was nice of you to share your toy with me." My heart would swell knowing that they were repeating things they had heard Willie and me say. They were mimicking the behavior they had seen in us while talking to their younger siblings.

At one point when they were little, I wrote in my journal about John Luke's tickling Sadie on her belly and saying, "I love this soft belly." Then he'd pinch her cheeks and say, "I love these cute cheeks." Then he'd kiss her feet, saying, "I love these little feet." This was a little game I played with each of our kids when they were babies and toddlers. They would giggle and smile the entire time. Nothing is better than hearing your three-year-old playing like this with his little sister. Even now, I smile every time I think of it. If the way we had talked to our babies had been negative and unkind, we would have heard those words from the other room instead of the kind, loving things they did say to one another.

Is the Life You're Living True to How God Made You?

Now for the second question I posed: Are you living a life that's true to who you are and true to how God made you? I'm talking about being original, being content with and confident in who you are and how God made you. Sadie wrote an entire book on this subject.[1] When she was about five years old, Willie nicknamed her "The Original." Rebecca hadn't joined our family yet, but baby Bella had, so Sadie wasn't the only girl in the family anymore. Bella was the new "little sister," and Sadie was labeled "the original little sister." At that time Willie and I were starting to realize how God had truly created each one of our children uniquely and beautifully different. From the time they were born, everything— from whether they liked to be rocked to sleep and how they liked to be held, to whether they liked to ride in their car seat and the shape of their fingernails and tiny earlobes—was unique in each of our children. If you have more than one child, you'll understand this completely.

If you're a new parent, you might be tempted to think that after the first child, you'll have the baby thing down. Your plan might be to do the exact same thing with child number two that you did with child number one. It certainly makes sense. You should be good to go. *I've got this*, you tell yourself. Then you have child number two, and everything is different. Not only is the one-of-a-kind little footprint they stamped in the hospital unique to the little one you'll be bringing home, but every single thing about that sweet little baby is unique. Just thinking about this fills me with wonder at a God who, in His infinite power, can make millions and millions of humans who basically have the same two eyes, two ears, mouth, nose, and bodies, yet each one of us is so uniquely and wonderfully made. On top of that, God gives each creation different personalities and talents. When Willie started calling Sadie "The Original," we had no idea how true those words would be. Sadie has lived up to her name and loves to tell others about being confident in who they are and who God made them to be. The truth is that all of our kids are originals—and so are yours. And the same goes for you, Mom and Dad.

No one else is just like you, with your character traits and lifetime of experiences. God made you for a reason. He loves you just the way you are and wants you to love yourself just the way you are as well. As I mentioned before, Jesus said that the greatest commandment is to love God with all your heart, and the second greatest is to love your neighbor as yourself (Matt. 22:36–40). We must love God and love who He has created us to be if we are to be able to love our neighbor fully and completely as Jesus calls us to do.

Not loving ourselves can lead us to be unkind to ourselves; unforgiving of our own mistakes; and jealous, covetous, and judgmental of others. How many of us have a running commentary going in our heads of all the things we want to change about ourselves? And how many of us say these things in front of our children? We try to teach our kids to be confident and positive about the way God made them, yet every time we look in the mirror, we wish—out loud—that our butts weren't so big, our hair wasn't so thin, and on and on. Even worse, we talk about the talents and gifts that we haven't been blessed with. We compare ourselves to others, sending a message to our kids that we're discontent with where we are in life or jealous that the promotion or the big house down the street went to someone else. None of these qualities are admirable, and we don't want to see them in our children.

If our children hear us voicing discontent with the way God made us or the life He has for us, then how can we expect them to be confident of God's plan for their life? We must model confident behavior for our children to be confident themselves. Even if we don't always feel it. I started to write, "Fake it till you make it," but then I deleted it, thinking, *Wait! This chapter is about being real. How can I tell people to fake it in a chapter about being real?* Okay, so what I'm saying is this: you've got to get yourself there, so if you have to shut your mouth and not say what you really feel about your thighs in front of your kids until you actually come to the point where you really love your thighs, then so be it. Children don't need a running commentary of the bad things in your life. Many years ago, I learned about the two lists. Have you heard about them? That's what each of us wakes up to every morning: a good list and a bad list. We have to decide which list we're going to focus on.

If you're struggling—if you find yourself complaining more than thanking—how can you get to a place where you're happy about who you are and the life you're living? Have you read Proverbs 23:7 in the King James Version? It's a great verse: "As he thinketh in his heart, so is he." To put it more simply, "you are what you think." There are tons of verses about being confident as God's children. One I love is found in Philippians 1:6: "Being confident of this, that he who began a good work in you will carry it on to completion until the day of Christ Jesus." If you struggle with being confident in God and His plan for you, memorize this verse and use it to replace any negative thoughts you might have. I promise that it will make a difference in how you love yourself, and that will overflow to others. Be confident in God's plan for your life.

I have one more story for you on this subject. This is an old Indian story called the "Tale of Two Wolves."

One evening, an elderly Cherokee brave told his grandson about a battle that goes on inside people. He said, "My son, the battle is between two 'wolves' inside us all. One is evil. It is anger, envy, jealousy, sorrow, regret, greed, arrogance, self-pity, guilt, resentment, inferiority, lies, false pride, superiority, and ego. The other is good. It is joy, peace, love, hope, serenity, humility, kindness, benevolence, empathy, generosity, truth, compassion, and faith."

The grandson thought about it and then asked his grandfather, "Which wolf wins?"

The old Cherokee replied, "The one that you feed."[2]

It seems like a simple solution, but if you will continually feed the good wolf, you'll become confident of the real person God created you to be.

ARE YOU ALLOWING YOUR KIDS TO SEE THAT BEING REAL CAN SOMETIMES BE MESSY?

As you can see, being real at home is a big topic. The last question I raised earlier was this: Are we allowing our kids to see that being real can sometimes be messy? I've encouraged you to create a home atmosphere where parents are who they say they are and who live out the values they are working to instill in their children. Now I want to tell you that it's okay for our kids to see us fail sometimes. In fact, they actually need to see this. The opposite of a home that has a perfect fake exterior but an ugly interior is the home with parents who work in overdrive to create the seemingly perfect life for their children at home *and* in the world. These are the kind of parents who don't want their children to ever experience pain or see them mess up; parents who control every situation for their children so that it all works out perfectly for them. They work behind the scenes to get the best teacher, to make sure that their kids' very best friends are in their cabins at summer camp, and to keep their kids from seeing any mistakes they may have made in the past.

An extreme example of this is the dad who loses his job but pretends to leave for work every morning because he doesn't want the kids to worry or know there's a problem. This kind of parenting doesn't prepare children for the real world. Life is tough. People make big mistakes. Parents lose their jobs and can't pay their bills. We overspend and get ourselves into debt. We argue with our spouses and say things we don't mean. We're not perfect, and life is not perfect. Letting our kids think that we are will set them up for future disappointment and disasters. Such a "perfect" home environment produces kids who think the world revolves around them and their needs. Wouldn't it be nice if it did? But it just doesn't. When these kids become teenagers, they'll quit the team when the coach criticizes them. They'll walk away from friends who make mistakes, struggle with employers who have high expectations for them, and bail out when their marriages cross a rough patch.

Another repercussion of not allowing kids to see that real life comes with real problems is that kids grow up thinking that their parents won't understand when the kids go through difficult times themselves. They might ask, "Why am I so flawed when my parents' lives seem so perfect?" Instead of reaching out to the ones who love them the most, they might turn to others who are not looking out for their best interests.

I know it's difficult to grasp the fact that allowing your kids to see your weaknesses is important. Who wants to disappoint their kids? Especially if, like me, one of the traits you value most is strength. However, they need to understand that being strong does not mean not failing or experiencing disappointments; it just means that we have the fortitude to get through those tough days. I recently realized that maybe I've been showing the strong side to my children and not allowing them to see my weaknesses quite enough.

If you watched *Dancing with the Stars* when Sadie was on it, you probably saw Willie crying. His eyes tend to get really watery when our kids do something he's proud of. Okay, we're both crybabies about our kids. I tend to cry when I talk about them, if I tell a story about something they did that really touched me, or if someone tells me about something good that they've done. The bottom line is that we cry when we're proud or happy, but Willie and I don't often cry when we're upset. We don't typically cry over a stubbed toe or a temporary disappointment. Because of this, our kids remember distinctly every time they've ever seen us cry.

This really hadn't hit me until a recent incident occurred that involved all of the children. I was recovering from a hysterectomy and the road to recovery had not been as smooth as I had hoped it would be. I'm one of those people who, when the doctor says, "You'll have to stay home for two weeks," thinks, *Oh, that will be nice. I'll get so much done. I'll organize my desk, work on my book, perhaps clean out closets . . .* I guess I was envisioning a vacation, not a recovery. I never dreamed it would be two weeks of getting out of my bed only to move to the recliner. When I went to my two-week checkup, I told the doctor that it had been worse than I'd expected. His comment was, "This is a major surgery. Even after six weeks, you'll only be 85 percent recovered."

"What?" I said in shock. "I'm ready to get back to normal life now!"

There were moments of bravery during this awful time. I had to do a couple of interviews for the television show, and I had to make one appearance. I managed to fake feeling good. And did I mention that I had surgery during the first week of December with Christmas right around the corner and not a single present bought? (I think somewhere I mentioned my lack of organizational skills. If not, I'll just say it now: I'm working on it.)

I hit my breaking point about two weeks into my recovery. I was frustrated about the fact that I wasn't feeling better yet; Willie was on a hunting trip; the kids were home all day because it was a Saturday; and I had stayed in bed most of the day. At lunchtime our sweet Will made me a sandwich, and John Luke made me a milkshake for a snack (ice cream is the way to my heart). So despite the fact that I felt bad, at least the kids were taking care of their mama.

That night, I woke up at three in the morning feeling thirsty and decided to go to the kitchen to get a glass of water. That's when I saw it! The house was destroyed. The bread, deli turkey, and deli cheese (from lunch, let me remind you) were sitting on the counter all dried out. Wait, there's more. The milk was still out from the milkshake John Luke had made me, and the counters were covered in mac-and-cheese boxes, soda cans, and chips bags. My house looked like a frat house after a party.

You have to know this before I go any further: I'm really not a neat freak. I'm totally okay with a house that looks lived in. People who know me can attest to the fact that I'm fine with people coming over without the house looking perfect. But leaving the food out on the counter to be ruined—well, that was it! I was beyond upset. I got back in bed and stewed for a minute. Then I shot off a text to the kids. (This text went to our family group message, affectionately titled by the kids "Swag Fam," where I usually say things like, "Goodnight, sweet kids. I love you and think you're the best!" and put in lots of kissy-face emojis.) Well, not this night. At 3:00 a.m. I sent a text to our kids that started with, "I have raised a bunch of slobs." It went on to say that they'd better come straight home from church that morning. Furthermore, they were not to even stop to eat; they needed to get home and clean up every bit of the mess. Then we were going to have a serious talk. I even used what Sadie calls "the D word"—*disappointed*. For Sadie, the worst thing she can hear is that her parents are disappointed in something she did. I did feel a little bad about calling them slobs, so I followed it up with a text saying that I was proud of them in so many ways, but that I really needed them to step it up in this department.

Well, the kids came in solemnly, one by one, in a line, after church. I'm sure they hoped that I would be over it by that time, but no, I was still pretty worked up about it. I had spent the morning thinking of all the ways I had failed as a mom. My disappointment was not just in my children, but in myself for not teaching them well enough. (I think it's important to note that Willie said a dad would never feel this way; he would never take the responsibility on himself that way. But that's what moms do.)

I was upset and not feeling well. In any case, I cried during our little family meeting that day. I apologized for the middle-of-the-night text calling them slobs; perhaps I could have handled that a little more calmly. I went on to explain that I was disappointed in the lack of care for the food we have and the home we have. We discussed how they could and would do better going forward. Then I made the kids clean up the entire house. We are now able to laugh about the whole incident, which I love. Every time I say anything about cleaning up, Sadie says in a dramatic voice, "What are we? A bunch of slobs!" and we all get a good laugh out of it.

Bella later told me that she knew this was serious because the last time she saw me upset and crying was when we were still living in our other house. We've been in the house we're in now for eight years, which means that she couldn't have been more than four years old. Still, she remembered everything about that particular event. Certainly, I've cried in the past eight years over stress, disappointment, heartache, and exhaustion. Apparently, Bella hadn't seen it.

I say all of this to say that it's okay for the kids to see us having those moments; perhaps I should show my kids those moments a bit more often. It's okay for your kids to see you vulnerable, for them to see that we all have times when we've just had enough, times when life gets overwhelming and people or circumstances disappoint us. That's part of being real with your kids.

Another way Willie and I try to keep it real with our kids is in our relationship. Most of the time we're very loving toward each other in front of our children. They see us kiss, hug, and laugh together; but there are also plenty of times when they see us argue and disagree. We don't hide that from our kids completely. We do work hard to save disagreements about their discipline or care for when they aren't around. We believe it's important to provide a united front concerning them and their discipline, but other things are fair game for disagreeing or arguing about in front of our kids. It's a way for them to learn how to disagree and argue with respect for one another, which is something they need to learn. If as parents we keep all of our disagreements to ourselves, then our children may have a false sense that marriages should be argument-free. Instead, they need to learn how to argue and stay together, how to resolve conflict, and sometimes to agree to disagree and move on. They need to know when to fight for what they believe in, when to compromise, and when to yield to their spouse's decision. They'll never learn these things if you save all of your arguments for behind closed doors. Of course, I'm not talking about knock-down, drag-out fights. I'm talking about disagreements where each partner is allowed to express his or her side of the argument.

BEING PERFECT ISN'T AS IMPORTANT AS BEING REAL

Life can be hard. It's important to have wisdom in knowing what is appropriate to share with our children as they grow older. But we should never pretend that hard days don't happen. Our kids usually see it anyway, and pretending doesn't make it go away. It's only a matter of time before they'll face tough days themselves. Showing them how you deal with tough times is, perhaps, the best way you can help them through it.

Willie's Words on Being Real

With the Robertsons what you see is what you get. People ask me all the time if Uncle Si is really the way they see him on television, and my response is always, "You can't fake that." Our family has always been an open book. We aren't afraid to say what's on our mind, and we don't shy away from telling the good, the bad, and the ugly about our lives.

I think that's the key to my relationship with my parents and our kids' relationship with us. I know my parents aren't perfect, and our kids know we aren't either. It gives us a greater freedom to talk about our problems and admit to rough times in our lives. When we started *Duck Dynasty*, people would say to us, "Don't you hate having the whole film crew in your home and cameras in your face all the time?" But for us, it didn't seem like that big of a deal. We've always had an open home with lots of friends and family in and out and someone sleeping on the couch if need be. We are who we are—love us or hate us, there's no faking it. Ephesians 5:8–13 says, "For you were once darkness, but now you are light in the Lord. Live as children of light (for the fruit of the light consists in all goodness, righteousness and truth) and find out what pleases the Lord. Have nothing to do with the fruitless deeds of darkness, but rather expose them. It is shameful even to mention what the disobedient do in secret. But everything exposed by the light becomes visible—and everything that is illuminated becomes a light."

When we keep our bad deeds hidden in darkness, there is no way for them to be resolved or healed. Being real means not being afraid to be exposed to the light. It is in this light that our lives become pleasing to God, and we can have the hope of helping to point others to Him.

TWENTY-ONE

BE UNIFIED

The first time I went to Willie's house was my first glimpse into how differently we were raised. I was in fifth grade. I hadn't seen him since the summer of my third grade year at Camp Ch-Yo-Ca when he had asked me to walk with him on the moonlight hike. Yes, Willie was my first crush. Who could resist those dimples and that smile? He was funny even then. Of course, two years later, I was very excited to be asked by my best friend to go to his house for dinner. My friend's parents had been invited to the Robertsons' house for a fish fry. Phil was commercial fishing during those days to make ends meet, so a fish fry was a pretty regular event. Like most fifth grade girls, my friend didn't want to go alone, so she asked me. It was my lucky day!

My friend and I walked into Phil and Miss Kay's home. (This is the home that is shown on TV now; only then it was about half the size. They have added on since I first visited many years ago.) This big, bearded man came up to us and, with a gruff voice, introduced himself as Phil Robertson. Then he asked if we had met his boys, Jason Silas and Willie Jess. He went on to tell us that they would make good husbands someday. He explained that they were good hunters and fishermen, so they would be good providers. *Whoa! I'm only in fifth grade*, I thought. Even though I wasn't thinking about a husband at the time, I did think Willie was the cutest thing I'd ever seen.

So back to the differences between our two families. Like Phil, my dad had a beard. At least at first glance, that was about all they had in common. My dad's beard was neatly trimmed. Let's just say that Phil's was not. My dad was a businessman who wore suits to work. Phil rarely put on shoes. While I did grow up fishing for bream and catfish in the pond behind our house, the only time I remember my dad going hunting was on a business trip. Our family owned a chain of retail stores. The company was the top seller of ammunition, so the ammo company took my dad and some other bigwigs on a hunting trip to South America. Other than that, I can't remember my dad ever talking about hunting, whereas hunting and fishing were the two things the Robertsons talked about daily.

Our moms were just as different as our dads. When I first met Miss Kay, she was in her small kitchen (about the size of our laundry room) covered in flour. I was nearly as tall as she was, even though I was just in fifth grade. I learned that she spent most of her time cooking for her family and all the Duck Commander employees. Since the company was run out of the Robertsons' home at that time, it was a perk for the employees to have Miss Kay's meals. On the other hand, my mom wasn't much of a cook. She jokes that she only has five recipes, and one of them is the phone number to the local pizza place. Her five solid meals are pretty classic recipes that every mom has to know—spaghetti, tacos, roast, and sloppy Joes. (Okay, I'm only remembering four—maybe she wasn't joking about the phone number to the pizza place.) Needless to say, cooking was not her calling. Her calling was kids.

During the school year, my mom taught in the special needs program at our school, and in the summer she was the director at Camp Ch-Yo-Ca. She went to all of our activities—the class mom and the ultimate party planner. She drove us to and from games and practices. She was always there cheering us on.

In Willie's family the kids didn't play organized sports until they were old enough to drive themselves or get a ride there. Willie's dad never attended one of his sporting events.

Every year on the first day of school, my mom drove us there, prayed with us at the flagpole, and documented it with pictures. (She still likes to do this with the grandkids, if we're all in town.) By contrast, Willie rode the bus on his first day of kindergarten.

The discipline techniques were different as well. The Robertson boys laughingly tell stories of Miss Kay chasing them around the house with a broomstick or turning her ring around to pop them on the head. I can't even imagine my mom chasing us around the house. It makes me laugh to think about it. Make no mistake: my mom was clearly in charge, but she wouldn't have popped us with her ring.

When I first met Willie, all of these things seemed so strange and foreign to me. Yet on closer inspection, I could see and feel the love, laughter, and respect in their home. They loved God and one another, just like the people in my home did. I loved everything about my family: the way our house was always open to friends and family; the way my dad would come to my softball games with his stack of mail and newspapers to read between plays; the way my mom helped us with our English papers and read to us at night. But I also loved hearing about the different way Willie grew up.

I've learned that there are many ways to raise a family—not right or wrong, just different. But this question always comes up: How do two people with totally different backgrounds become unified enough to raise healthy, happy children? To be unified is to make different pieces or parts into a unit or coherent whole. Isn't that what the Bible tells us is the ultimate plan of marriage, for two to become one? Ephesians 5:31 says, "'A man will leave his father and mother and be united to his wife, and the two will become one flesh.'"

How Can We Be United When We're So Different?

Okay, but how do we do that? How can we be united when we're so different? A good place to start is with tolerance—being willing to accept feelings, practices, or beliefs that are different from your own. Tolerance is important in a society. For me, tolerance is being okay with the fact that not everyone will think as I do and learning to accept the feelings, practices, and beliefs of others that are different from my own. In fact, more than just *accepting* that not everyone is going to think like me, it's *expecting* them not to.

One of the blessings of a big family is seeing this played out. In our family we have different beliefs about political issues and different ideas about childrearing. We go about our daily activities in different ways. If we weren't tolerant of our differences, we wouldn't all be able to live on the same street. (Right now, thirty-five family members live on our street.)

EXCEL IN SHOWING RESPECT

I think we can understand that God wants us to be tolerant by observing Jesus' example of the people He chose to spend His time with while here on earth (Matt. 11:19) and Paul's teaching in 1 Corinthians 9:22 to "become all things to all people" so that we may win them over to the gospel. But I believe that God is calling us to something even deeper than that. Paul tells us that Christians, as followers of God's Word, have a responsibility to do more than just tolerate others. In Romans 12, Paul wrote that we are one body with many members and that we should honor others above ourselves. He went on to say that Christians, as one translation puts it, should "excel in showing respect for each other" (v. 10 GW). It seems to me that the quest for becoming unified will require much more than simply being tolerant of each other.

Let's look again at one of the words used in Romans 12:10. It says we should *excel* in showing respect for each other. To excel means to be the best you can be. When we excel, we shine as we outclass, rival, top, and surpass what is expected. To me, that sounds like much more than tolerance.

I once heard someone say it this way: we shouldn't just love people in spite of their differences; we should love others because of them. I'll give it to you that we can tolerate the way our spouse squishes the toothpaste or has to search for his keys every morning because he never puts them in the same place twice. But in matters of greatest importance, it's critical that we do more than tolerate one another. We must excel in showing respect for one another.

Even when we don't agree with someone, we can still be respectful and show love. In Ephesians 5, right after he says, "'the two will become one'" (v. 31), Paul adds, "Each one of you also must love his wife as he loves himself, and the wife must respect her husband" (v. 33).

Love and respect are two key concepts necessary for a husband and wife to truly become one. In chapter 18 we discussed love as based on the Bible's definition in 1 Corinthians 13. If you've forgotten, go back and read that chapter again; it's worth the time.

Unity Comes from Respect

Now, let's talk about respect. The Bible has a lot to say about respect too. It tells us to respect one another and to respect our elders. It challenges us to live lives worthy of respect. *Merriam-Webster's Dictionary* includes these definitions of *respect*: "a feeling of admiring someone or something that is good, valuable, important, etc." and "a feeling or understanding that someone or something is important, serious, etc., and should be treated in an appropriate way."[1]

To have unity in our marriages, especially in raising our children, we need to respect our spouses in the sense of both of these definitions. If your spouse is easy to admire, it will be easy to treat him or her with respect in the sense of the first definition. It's easy to respect a spouse who is a genuinely good person with a pleasing personality. It's natural to respect someone who works hard, does a good job, and provides well for the family.

But maybe your spouse has a prickly personality, or maybe he's struggling to hold down a job. Perhaps he is going through some other difficulty that is distracting him or making him difficult to deal with. Not all spouses act admirably. When that's the case, the second definition of *respect* becomes even more important. It talks about "understanding that someone or something is important . . . and should be treated in an appropriate way." A wife is to respect her husband because of his role, even if his behavior isn't worthy of respect. Husbands must also respect their wives in this same way. It's critical for moms and dads to respect each other's position and treat each other kindly. This is not always easy, especially in cases of divorce, but even when a marriage has splintered, it's vital that parents present a unified front in raising the children and treat each other with respect. Respect is not just a naturally occurring feeling; it's an active acknowledgment of the importance of the other and an act of the will. You might say that respect has to have feet on it. It's something we can all choose to give to our husbands or wives, celebrating their lives and their importance in our own lives—even if we don't agree with them about everything.

Willie and I have always worked hard to treat each other with love and respect, and I think it's one of the reasons our marriage has been successful. We talk a lot about our hopes, dreams, wants, and needs for ourselves, for our children, and for our family. We listen to and work to respect each other in spite of our differences. We resist trying to make the other person into someone or something he or she is not; I don't try to make him more like my dad, and he doesn't try to make me be more like his mom. We treat each other like the adults we are, and we don't try to parent each other. We talk about things, but neither of us forces the other to ask permission before doing something (strangely, this seems to be common in some marriages).

I don't want you to think that all of this has come easily for us. Each of us came into our marriage with expectations of what our spouse would or wouldn't do or say. Like many newlyweds, when we discovered that our new spouse wasn't going to meet our expectations, we set about trying to change each other. However, after a few futile months of trying to make this happen, we realized that we were on a path to disunity. It's easy to become disrespectful and resentful of each other when you live with unmet expectations or when you can't live up to someone else's expectations for you. Trust me, we've been there, done that. Willie and I have come to realize that life is much better when we just treat each other the way we would want to be treated—with love and respect. We've been married for twenty-three years at the time of this writing and look forward to many more. We're not perfect, but we're doing many things right; one of them is celebrating our differences and respecting each other.

Be Unified in Front of the Children

I've told you about the many differences in Willie's and my families, but let me tell you how they're alike. First and foremost, both sets of parents love God and love each other. Furthermore, as parents, they presented united fronts to their children. I'm convinced this is critical to raising strong, healthy children. No matter the differences or difficulties in other aspects of our marriage, I've always had confidence that Willie will have my back when it comes to the kids. What's more, I believe he has confidence that I'll always have his. When Willie disciplines the children or makes a decision, he knows that I won't be rolling my eyes behind his back, and the children know that I won't go around him and let them off the hook. In the same way, when I tell the children to do something and they don't do it immediately or they talk back, Willie quickly lets them know their behavior isn't acceptable.

When I was growing up, my siblings and I would never have thought of being disrespectful to our mom because our dad wouldn't have stood for it, and it was the same way in Willie's home. I'm grateful to have seen this model of parental unity, and I'm grateful that Willie did as well. Our children have learned to respect me because their dad respects me, and the same goes for their respect for him.

Just for clarification, this doesn't mean that Willie blindly goes along with everything I say or do (if you've watched an episode of *Duck Dynasty*, you know this is not the case). But in matters of discipline and raising our children, we always support each other in front of our children. We don't play games in our family. No child goes from parent to parent looking for the answer he or she wants. This game is very harmful to children. While they think they want parents like this, they really don't. Children want parents who are unified. It gives them a feeling of security.

One more clarification: Willie and I don't always agree on discipline techniques, although after twenty years in the parenting business, we've come to think alike most of the time. But when we do disagree, we have that discussion behind closed doors. We talk, argue, come together, or agree to disagree in private—but in front of the children, on matters of discipline, we stand together. They see a unified front.

An example of this is happening as I write this book. Our Will has always been a smart kid. As I said earlier, he was our earliest talker and reader. I've told you a little about his early struggles with discipline in school. I truly believe that part of those struggles came because he was a very bright little man who was easily bored when school wasn't challenging. He has always made all As and Bs on his report card, but here we are in seventh grade and he recently came home with two Ds.

What? This shouldn't be happening. I know how smart this kid is. I went back and checked online (our school has all grades and assignments online) and discovered that his test grades were good, but there were zeros spread throughout the nine weeks. Our sweet Will simply wasn't doing his homework. Didn't I ask him every day if he had any homework? What are we going to do about it? Why would a kid just not do his homework? I asked Willie these questions and more (behind closed doors, of course), agonizing about where we had gone wrong.

What do you think Willie's response was based on how he was raised? I'll tell you: Willie said, "Let him fail. He's old enough to learn consequences the hard way. If he has to take seventh grade again, so be it." That's how his parents would have handled such a situation. Mine, on the other hand, would have had me with a tutor before I could turn around. So we talked it out. I told Willie that I couldn't let our child fail seventh grade. Willie asserted that Will was smarter than to let himself fail and chalked it up to "pure-D" (Southern term) laziness. I agreed and believed that Will should be punished, but I also wanted to get him help.

Willie knew that I felt more strongly about this than he did—he got by with average grades in high school and made it through college with a little help from his wife, so he really isn't the authority in the academic arena. So he agreed to go along with whatever I decided was right in this case. We decided on a punishment that included taking away all Will's electronics until his grades reached an acceptable level, and we hired a tutor to work with him two days a week. While it's not the way Willie's parents would have handled it, Willie trusted me and respected my opinion enough to go along with my plan and enforce the punishment that we agreed upon. I'm happy to report that Will finished out his seventh grade year much better than he started it, and I'm grateful that Willie could see my point of view, value it, and back me up by helping to enforce the discipline. Had he done anything less, Will would have sensed weakness and not taken his punishment and schoolwork seriously.

COMMIT TO UNITY IN PARENTING

If you are in the habit—and I do believe it can be a habit—of disrespecting your spouse and not honoring each other in your home, now is the time to make a change. Have a heart-to-heart talk with your spouse. If you're separated or divorced, this still applies. Children should not have to figure out where, when, and how the rules change. I know that kids survive this type of upbringing, but it's not the best. It breeds insecurity and frustration.

After you come together with your spouse and agree to support each other, bring in the kids—no matter how old they are. First, apologize to them for not respecting and honoring one another in your home, and tell them that from now on, things will be different. Tell them that moving forward you and your spouse will stand united and that they will be expected to honor whatever Mom or Dad asks of them. The main thing is to remember that children respect parents who stand together, support each other, and lovingly lead their children by example.

Respect breeds respect. When someone feels respected, he or she is much more likely to respect you in return. And when you respect each other, it's much easier to be unified in your decision-making. Showing respect says you trust the other person's decisions and are willing to back him or her up. Your home life will be much more pleasant, and someday your children will thank you if they are blessed to have parents who love each other enough to also respect them. Trust me, being unified is a worthy goal. Treat it as such.

Willie's Words on Being Unified

One of the things a couple really needs to get right is being unified. This is especially important when dealing with your children's behavior and discipline issues. This doesn't mean that you both don't have strengths in certain areas, but when it comes to how to handle a certain behavior, you have to agree on what is best. If a couple can't work together in this area, there might be other issues where they're not unified, and it signals trouble in the relationship. Of course, disagreements will pop up, but that should tell you it's time for communication and trust, not pulling away. After all, who should you trust more with raising your kids than your spouse?

There have been times when I thought a certain child deserved a pass, but Korie felt more strongly about the issue. When that happens, we have to talk it out. Once we're on the same page, we go present that to the child. It would be crazy to think we would agree every time on every issue, but we can agree to disagree and then come up with a solution that works for both of us.

In twenty-three years of marriage, this is an area I think we've gotten right. We've stood rock-solid as a parenting team. Our goal is to be in heaven with our children and for them to live on earth as strong and kind people. If we keep our goals in mind and don't let our egos rule, we'll make the right decisions. This means that even after the fact, if the situation didn't work out like you wanted it to, you don't come back with, "I told you so." Remember, you committed to "until death do you part" with your spouse, and you brought this child into the world together. What each of you thinks really does matter, but in some instances, someone's opinion has to get top priority. That's when each parent has to be willing to step aside for the good of the child.

Korie and I could not have been raised more differently. My parents were laid-back, not very involved, and, shall I say, a bit rough. Korie's parents were hands-on and involved, set curfews, and gave allowances. Korie went to private school, and I went to public school. Korie was salutatorian of her senior class; my parents didn't really care if we walked across the stage with cap and gown or not. In fact, Jase just told them to mail his diploma to him. The reason I say all this is to say that it doesn't matter how differently you were raised. We both came out fine, and the fact that we are unified in how we raise our kids is a testament to our commitment and faith.

There are times when I need to use my street-smart, hard upbringing and times when the situation calls for Korie's more organized, goal-oriented consistency. All of these qualities give strength to our parenting team. Both of our families had the most important thing in common—they love God and each other. We appreciate our parents and how they raised us. We realize that not everything they did was perfect, and we won't be perfect either. But our faith in God, our trust in each other, and our desire to be consistent will keep us unified.

TWENTY-TWO

BE CREATIVE

When Rebecca came to live with us, at the age of sixteen, she brought with her some treats from Taiwan: a thousand-year-old egg that tasted exactly how you would imagine it would taste, dried fish sticks that she ate out of a bag like popcorn and smelled worse than you can imagine, a box of ribbons, and green tape and wire that I had no idea what she planned to do with or why they had made their way into her overstuffed suitcase. She joined our family in August 2004, and by the time Mother's Day came around in May 2005, she had become like one of ours. I had pried her fingers off of my arm the first day of school like a nervous kindergartner and read books from the library to her every night because she could hardly speak a word of English. She had taught us to count in Chinese and taught Sadie a Taiwanese rap song. On that first Mother's Day with us, Rebecca surprised me with a beautiful bouquet of flowers made out of that ribbon, tape, and wire that she had brought all the way from Taiwan. Seeing the intricate detail of what she created, I knew she had spent many hours in her room at night making this elaborate bouquet. She could have gone to the store and bought me flowers, but what she created was much more special.

We've been made in the image of an incredibly imaginative Creator. Don't you love all the fun little details God put into creating us and our amazing planet? Take some time to search for "Amazing Things God Made" on Pinterest. Not only will you see a lot of creativity, but you'll also see that God has a great sense of humor. Some of those sea creatures are hilarious to look at. We are made in the image of One who is very creative, so we must be creative, too, right? Right. You have no excuse.

This chapter is about inspiring you to think of parenting not simply as a chore to be done but as an opportunity for a creative adventure. With a little encouragement, you'll come up with some ways to make parenting fun for your children as well as yourself. Your children will fall in love with the One who created them by falling in love with you, their earthly parents, as you creatively love and discipline them, being a living example of how God loves and disciplines us.

Take Delight in Your Kids

I chose to put this chapter toward the end for a reason. Many times we get so caught up in being consistent, confident, honest, and all those things we've discussed in previous chapters that we forget to have fun. Then parenting can feel like a chore rather than the gift it is. Our children might get the sense that they're causing us problems rather than bringing us joy.

Psalm 149:4 tells us that "the Lord takes delight in his people." We should take delight in our people—our children—as well and let them know it. Have you ever complimented someone else's child only to have his mother reply, "Yeah, he's cute, but he's a brat." This makes me cringe! We should be saying good things about our children rather than making them feel like troublemakers that we tolerate more than love. We should clearly communicate that they are worthy of our time and creative energies.

In Psalm 139:13–16, the writer marvels at the care God took in creating him.

> You created my inmost being;
>> you knit me together in my mother's womb.
> I praise you because I am fearfully and wonderfully made;
>> your works are wonderful,

I know that full well.
My frame was not hidden from you
    when I was made in the secret place,
    when I was woven together in the depths of the earth.
Your eyes saw my unformed body;
    all the days ordained for me were written in your book
    before one of them came to be.

God took equal time and care when creating each of us and each of our children. We must be equally committed to using our creativity to raise our children with great care to be the best they can be and to give God the glory and honor He deserves.

The Importance of Talking to Your Children

Recently, I read a study about the importance of talking to your children. It was based on the research of Betty Hart and Todd R. Risley of the University of Kansas, who in 1995 published the book *Meaningful Differences in the Everyday Experience of Young American Children.* Hart and Risley studied how parents of different socioeconomic backgrounds talked to their babies. They studied forty-two families, recording an hour of parent-child interaction each month. They studied what they talked about, whether the talk was positive or negative, and *how much* parents praised their children. Then, when the children were nine years old, they picked up the study, examining how well the kids were doing in school. It wasn't until they had collected the data that they realized that the important variable was *how much* talking the parents were doing.[1]

The study uncovered vast differences in the amount of parental interaction with their children; some children heard only six hundred words per hour from their parents or caregivers while in other families the parents said up to twenty-one hundred words to their children in an hour. The study found that the greater the number of words children heard from their parents or caregivers before they were three, the higher their IQ and the better they did in school.[2]

For some of you, talking to your children may come easily, but others might have grown up in a home without much interaction and, before reading this, you didn't realize how important it is. Don't punish yourself for what you haven't done; just start now.

What Can You Talk About with Kids?

What is worthy of talking about with your child? What isn't! Give your baby or child a running commentary about your daily life. When they are babies, try simple things, like pointing out body parts, animal sounds, shapes, and colors. When our children were very young, we played little games with them, saying, "How big is Will?" He would raise his hands up high in the air, and we'd say, "Sooo big!" Or we would say, "Show me your muscles," and cute little Bella would strain to tighten her tiny muscles. We'd make silly faces together: surprised face, sad face, happy face, and so on. It's amazing at what a young age babies can learn these simple little games. I don't have any babies anymore, but we are still surrounded by cousins' babies. Recently, at a family gathering, our toddlers were playing the Who Is That? game. You know, the game where you point to each family member and say, "Who is that?" Trust me, in our big family we have to do this often so our new little ones can get to know all of their family members.

Another game I loved to play with our children when they got a little older was I Spy. This game can be played anytime or anywhere. When you're in the car or at home or waiting in a busy doctor's office, you can take turns spying colors, objects, numbers, or letters. Easy rhyming games are fun for children too. Say a word, and then ask your child to think of as many words as he can that rhyme. Then let him be the leader and come up with a word for you to rhyme.

When I was little, my grandmother taught me a game that my family still loves to play. Our kids today call it the Song Game (I know—really creative title). Someone comes up with a word, and then everyone takes turns thinking of a song that has that word in it. The one who comes up with the most songs with that word in it wins the round and gets to choose the next word. We also loved a game called Fortunately and Unfortunately. Someone starts off a story with a sentence, such as, "Once upon a time, there was a prince." The next person must start the next sentence with the word *fortunately*. For example, "Fortunately, the prince lived in a giant castle." The next person starts the following sentence with the word *unfortunately*: "Unfortunately, the castle was surrounded by dragons." The next sentence starts with *fortunately*, and you keep alternating until the story is completed. You can come up with some pretty creative stories by doing this; plus, you might discover a budding author.

I've already mentioned our game of Highs and Lows. This is a mealtime favorite at my mom's house. If all the cousins are there, someone will say, "Let's tell Highs and Lows." This is a great way to get everyone talking and, equally important, everyone listening. Each person gets to share a good thing about the day and, if he or she wants to, a bad thing.

Many cars have DVD players in them now, but this didn't become popular until our younger two were born. Eventually, we got a minivan that had one, but we made a rule that it was only to be used on long road trips. (I'll admit this was a lifesaver when we drove to the beach every year. I was actually able to read a book while Willie drove and the kids watched a movie in the back.) However, when we were just driving around town, it was our time to talk, play games, and interact with one another, rather than watching fifteen minutes of *The Little Mermaid*, or whatever Disney movie they loved at the time. My suggestion is to enjoy this invention, but to use it wisely. It certainly can be helpful on a long trip. Just don't let it become the babysitter on a regular basis.

CREATIVE GAMES TO PLAY WITH YOUR KIDS

Some of these games are just for fun, some are for learning to think creatively, and some are for teaching lessons. A few below are fun for kids while also teaching lessons. I personally believe that games such as Mother May I? and Simon Says came from creative moms looking for ways to teach obedience. If any of you know the actual origin of those games, feel free to let me know, but for now I'm going to believe a wise mom was behind those fun games.

Mother May I?

If you're not familiar with the game Mother May I? (because it's an old one, and electronics have taken over our game-playing time), here's a brief explanation. Children line up in a straight line facing but several feet away from the "mother," played by another child. The mother calls out an instruction such as, "Take two giant steps," or "Hop three times," to one of the "children," and before moving toward the mother in accordance with her direction, the child asks, "Mother may I?" When the child asks, "Mother may I?" the mother replies, "Yes, you may," and the child completes the task. If he fails to say those words, he has to go back to the starting line. The goal is to be the first to reach the mother. You can see how this game would teach a child to respectfully ask for mom's permission.

Red Light/Yellow Light/Green Light

You can probably understand the gist of Red Light/Yellow Light/ Green Light just from its title. Position the children a good distance away from you and, when you say "Green light," they should run toward you. Say "Yellow light" when you want them to walk slowly, and "Red light" when you want them to stop. If they don't follow your instructions immediately, they have to go back to where they started out. The first one to reach you wins. This is one of those games that I felt could have literally saved my children's lives. I think all moms fear that their children will run into the path of a moving car or take off in a crowd and become lost. When the kids were small, we'd talk about this before we got out of the car in a busy parking lot; then we'd play this game all the way to the store. I'd also mix in "Stop," "Slow," and "Go" commands to the game so that if I said "Stop," they'd do so immediately, as well as if they heard the command "Red light."

What Would You Do?

What Would You Do? is a multiple-choice game that I played with our kids when they were young. They loved it, and it taught them valuable lessons about making good choices. I would ask them fun questions like: "If you had to eat one thing every day for the rest of your life, which would you choose: (a) pizza, (b) macaroni and cheese, or (c) ice cream?" Then I would mix in more serious questions such as these: "If your friends were being mean to someone, what would you do: (a) be mean too, (b) do nothing, or (c) ask them to stop?" Or "If someone you don't know asks you to go somewhere with him to see a puppy, what would you do: (a) go with him because you like puppies, (b) say "no thank you" and go tell mom, or (c) ask him where the dog is?" This can be tailored to any age and can lead to important discussions about making good choices.

Being creative is all about just putting a little extra time into making your home a pleasant place to come back to. I purposely didn't use the word *fun* because that might scare a few of you into thinking you'll have to have a dance party every night, which isn't my intention (although I think it's important for our home life to be fun, and a good dance party every once in a while never hurt anyone). Don't worry, neither am I talking about searching the Internet for the latest creative way to make pancakes that look exactly like Yoda (I actually saw that tutorial video on Facebook) or waking up your kids with a joke every day (I always forget the punch line). Instead, I'm talking about doing little things that make your home a place where your family feels loved, safe, joyful, and, yes, happy. I'm also talking about making teaching, learning, and even discipline fun.

BE CREATIVE IN DISCIPLINE

Creative discipline can be as elaborate as a chore and obedience chart that you make with your kids or as simple as asking them to follow fun commands, like dropping and giving you ten push-ups when their energy is a little over the top and needs direction rather than sending them to another time-out.

Once, when I was at the end of my rope with four little ones who had seemingly been fighting and destroying the house all day, Willie walked into the house. I was in the kitchen washing dishes, and the kids were arguing in the living room with the television blaring. I let him know immediately what had been going on, and he simply walked across the room and turned off the TV. The silence caught their attention. Willie didn't have to say anything; no yelling was involved, and there were no dramatic speeches about their behavior. That was all it took. The kids immediately sobered up and started playing together quietly. It was like magic. After that, I used this technique often. It even worked in the car: if the kids were arguing over which station to listen to or where we were going to eat lunch, I would simply turn off the radio, and we would sit in silence until they decided to behave. Somehow, it worked every time. This is an example of creative discipline; it's not something you're going to find on Pinterest, but it's effective and not your usual time-out chair.

LEARN TO LAUGH AT
YOURSELVES—AND HAVE FUN!

I'm blessed to have a husband who is a funny guy. I don't take this for granted. It doesn't matter what's going on in our home—be it an extra-cranky child or a broken major appliance—Willie will say something to make us laugh. When our kids were young, if one of them was crying about something ridiculous, Willie would sing the Boyz II Men song "It's So Hard to Say Goodbye to Yesterday," but he would change the words to "It's So Hard to Be a Kid Today" and sing it in a soft falsetto voice that made us all laugh. Before long, the crying child would have forgotten why he or she was crying in the first place and joined our laughing.

Learning to laugh at yourself and not take yourself too seriously is truly an important lesson every child should learn. This ability is essential in the Robertson family; children quickly learn that life is a whole lot more fun if you can laugh at yourself. This comes more easily for some than for others, but I promise you: this life will be much easier and more fun if you learn not to take yourself so seriously that you can't laugh with others.

Our family has lots of fun traditions and activities we do to have fun together, but this will undoubtedly look different for your family. Creativity means using your imagination to come up with original ideas; I can't tell you how to be creative, but I can remind you that you were made in the image of the ultimate Creator. For this reason, being creative is within you; tap into this part of yourself to help grow happy, healthy kids.

Willie's Words on Being Creative

I love creativity. Creativity has no ceilings, no limits, and no shape. It starts small and then grows. It brings others in, grabs ideas and thoughts, and then, like a snowball rolling down a snow-covered mountain, it grows. It may get funnier, become deeper, or just add layers upon layers.

Sitting around a table with really creative people is one of the things I really enjoy doing. I have many creative friends, some I knew before *Duck Dynasty* and some I have met since our TV show. They express their creativity through different genres—music, theater, movies, TV, cooking, business, and many other areas.

I have been able to produce many TV shows, and the best part is being able to be creative. It's fun to take a simple idea and watch it grow into a show. As an employer I love hiring creative people. One of the most creative guys I know is a guy named Skip. Skip is a carpenter who builds for me. And when I say builds for me, I mean just that. He builds stuff. He can build anything. He can see an old barn that has caved in and think, *I could make that into a beautiful cabinet with wood ducks sitting on it*. One of the best things about being creative is you don't have to have degrees in creativity. Creativity is a God-given gift.

My love for creativity affects how I want to raise my children. It's fun to think and dream of how your child might influence the world, but you never know what area that particular child might be creative in. It could be something you never dreamed about—totally unlike you. Korie and I have watched different ones of ours do something funny or smart or creative and won-dered, *Is this what they are going to do?* Once, when I was a kid, I brought in a huge stereo and put it in front of Phil. I turned the music on and did a total breakdance. I'm still not sure what Phil was thinking, but he gave me the ol' thumbs-up. Well, breakdancing wasn't my calling, and I sure wish there were cell phones back then because I would love to see that dance today.

I think at the heart of being creative is taking time to think, and then it takes hard work to bring anything creative to life. When I see my kids playing video games, to me that's just being lazy and there's not a whole lot of creativity happening at that moment. That's when we have to set limits on activities like video games and encourage our kids to be creative.

We also have to be open to the fact that creativity can come in many different forms. This might sound funny to you, but as a kid, I was creative with yard work. Yes, I said yard work. One of my earliest memories is standing in front of a huge burn pile. I had raked the leaves and sticks into a pile and built a major fire. My mom was at work and my dad was teaching school at that time, so my granny was in charge. I was four years old at the time. At the dinner table that night (yes, we've ended our day at the dinner table for a long time) the family bragged on Willie J for cleaning the whole yard and burning it up. That was a different time, and I sure don't recommend letting your four-year-old burn the leaves, but I'm thankful for the memory of my family supporting my creativity.

That was just the beginning of my impressive cleaning and designing yard skills. I'm sure it came from my desire to please my mom and wanting people to pull up to our house and be impressed by our yard. As I got older, I would build flowerbeds, lay stepping stones, and use anything I could to make our yard look cool. The first year that I was on staff at Duck Commander, I did landscaping. I put in a stone courtyard, a cross-tie stairway, and a fountain that are still there today. I really loved using my creativity that way. It would have been natural for me to go that direction for my life job, but you never know where God is going to take you or your children. The main thing was I was willing to work and willing to think. Maybe all that time working in the yard gave me time to think about other things, like a TV show.

I count it such a privilege to watch our children be creative. I'll start with John Luke. Wow, this kid does not live in a box! (I'm sure Phil felt the same way when he saw me breakdance.) I've seen John Luke do so many creative things that I have no idea what he will do in life. By the way, that's great. I don't have to have it all worked out in my mind or try to lay a path out for him. Just let it go where it goes. When Sadie was on *Dancing with the Stars*, I got to see, along with America, how creative this girl is. She also uses her creativity to show others that she loves and appreciates them. I love that. Will is so musically creative. I hear his random beats that he can make with his mouth and realize that's another level of creativity that not everyone can do. Then there's Bella, who loves to cook and create like I do in the kitchen, but she's also a very funny storyteller with a Robertson knack for entertaining. Rebecca is so creative in the fashion world. It's amazing how she can see colors and combinations. She might be the next Coco Chanel. I really don't have a clue what they will do in life, but I know they are creative, and I will always foster that creativity and encourage them to work hard at whatever they choose to do. I'm not sure my dad knew my future would be in TV, but that breakdance had to have given him a clue.

TWENTY-THREE

BE INTENTIONAL

When I was young, I thought I understood what it means to be intentional. In high school I got my homework done while the teacher was still teaching class so I didn't have to do it at home. In college I decided on my major before starting my freshman year and breezed through just as I had intended. I never changed my major and don't remember ever dropping a class. I really enjoyed school and was intent upon sailing through with flying colors. As intentional as I am, as I said in chapter 17, I also enjoy being spontaneous and never like to have my days totally planned out.

My mom has always said I'm a bit of a strange breed. I've got some of the typical firstborn tendencies of being a good student, motivated, and responsible, but in the areas of organization and planning, not so much. I grew up with a mom who is much more of a planner than I am. It used to drive her crazy when we didn't have plans—after all, we couldn't just have nothing planned on a day off! Mom always wanted to plan an activity, go to the park, play tennis, or invite friends over—just do *something*. (She and Sadie are soul sisters in this area.)

And don't get me started on taking road trips with her. For Mom, it's all about getting to the destination while Willie and I will stop to eat or shop along the way. When Willie and I went to school in Italy for a semester in college, we'd hop on the Eurorail every weekend and travel around Europe. We were lost most of the time because, for us, it was more about the adventure than about the destination. We finally learned to hang out with others in our group who were planners so we wouldn't miss something great because we failed to plan—but without actually having to plan trips ourselves. Hey, it worked!

However, when I transitioned from college life to life as a young mother with a newborn baby, I had every ambition of being just as intentional about raising this new little baby as I had been about my schoolwork. As I mentioned earlier, as with all new moms, I soon discovered that it's really hard to be intentional on 2.2 hours of sleep. In fact, you quickly abandon intentional mode and go into crisis mode. *What do I absolutely have to do right now for this baby to survive—and stop crying?* Taking care of a newborn is all about the needs of the moment. When John Luke cried, I fed him. When he had a dirty diaper, I changed him. When he cried for no apparent reason, I rocked him. That's how it goes for a while. You just fill the need as it comes, give as much love and sweet forehead kisses as humanly possible, and wake up in a few hours and do it again.

I still tried to be at least somewhat intentional during this time— every day, I intended to get a shower and get out of my pajamas at some point. This reactive phase doesn't last long, though. Those sweet days of snuggling with our little time suckers, barely able to tend to their immediate needs, are soon gone. That's when the real work of being an intentional parent begins.

Why Is It Important to Be an Intentional Parent?

So what is an intentional parent, and why is it important to be one? Being intentional means that you do things on purpose, deliberately, and with forethought and planning. Based on what I've told you about myself you should know that when I'm talking about being intentional, I'm not talking about planning every second of your child's day. As a matter of fact, I think that parents usually do too much of that these days. Instead, I'm talking about being purposeful.

This is really the core of what this book is about. I've asked you to think about what you want for your children and to intentionally do those things that will get them there. All of this intentionality is no guarantee that life with your children will always be smooth sailing, but the values and traits you want to plant in your children are much more likely to grow if you are intentional about cultivating them. We read earlier the proverb that says, "Train up a child in the way he should go: and when he is old, he will not depart from it" (Prov. 22:6 KJV). You have to decide where you want your child to end up if you are to be successful in training him up and pointing him in that direction. Being intentional is the first step in this process.

THE FREEDOM OF PLANNING AHEAD

Earlier I talked about the importance of showing love during the process of building a new home. During our married life, Willie and I have built three homes and I've loved every one of them. Building a house entails making a gazillion decisions, and it can become a full-time job if you're not careful. I'm like most of you—a busy working wife and mother. I don't have time to make building a house my full-time job. One of the most important lessons I've learned from trial and error while building our homes is that the more you plan ahead and the better you plan, the more smoothly the process goes and the more you enjoy it. When building a home, if you wait till the last minute to make decisions, change your mind about what you like, and wait for someone to ask before you choose the next color or tile, you'll end up way over budget and way off schedule.

When we were building our current home (it's the last one, honey—I promise!), I was intentional about planning nearly everything before we broke ground. It took more than a year of planning and meeting with the architects and designers to get the plans just right before we even began the building process. But once we broke ground, from start to finish our new home took only a little over a year to build, and I can honestly say the weather was the only thing we had to wait for in the process. Things went smoothly, Willie and I got along swimmingly the entire time, and we were only a little bit over budget.

Our God is purposeful. He didn't just put things into motion and walk away. He continues to be an active partner in our lives. The second-most popular Bible verse on BibleGateway.com (John 3:16 is the first one) is Jeremiah 29:11, which reminds us of this: "'I know the *plans* I have for you,' declares the LORD, '*plans* to prosper you and not to harm you, *plans* to give you hope and a future.'" Why do you think this verse is so well loved? We all like to know that God, our heavenly Father, has good plans for us, that He is thinking about us, dreaming good things for our future, and that we are safe to trust in His plans for us because He is planning with our best interests in mind. The word *plans* is used three times in that verse. Yes, our God is intentional. Our heavenly Father has plans for us that we can trust, just as earthly parents have good plans for their children.

AN EXAMPLE OF LIVING INTENTIONALLY—MAMAW JO

You can't pursue a goal without being intentional. My sweet Mamaw Jo recently has decided to retire at the age of eighty-four by selling her real estate business. She was so used to working full-time that she questioned whether retiring made good sense. She wondered what she would do to fill her days. She explained, "I like having something to work toward every day, something to get up and get dressed for." I'm so inspired by Mamaw Jo's desire to stay active and pursue daily goals. Even at her age she didn't back away from joining the new world of social media. She keeps up with us on Facebook, Twitter, and Instagram. She was never content to do business the old way but updated her systems to include online billing and advertising. She never stopped learning and growing.

Every Christmas we gather at Mamaw's house for Christmas brunch. Mamaw spends three days cooking everything from sticky buns and egg casseroles to bananas Foster for our large family. Before we leave her house, we all crowd out on her deck for the annual "grandkid picture with Mamaw." In last year's picture, forty-one grandkids and great-grandkids—smiling and full of biscuits and sticky buns—surrounded Mamaw Jo. You'd think that she'd say, "I'm done," that all that she had accomplished would be enough, but it's not. Her desire to do more is inspiring. Mamaw sings in the church choir, hosts a Sunday night house church, bakes cakes at a moment's notice, is a mentor mom in our church's mentoring program, and attends nearly every grandchild's sporting events. Although she says she's retiring, she still can be found at the real estate office several days a week, helping with the transition. Mamaw Jo has always been intentional about her family. She works to make sure her children and grandchildren know how much she loves them and is there for them.

Last year we were having a party for John Luke's class, and I had offered to do the after-party that would start at 11:00 p.m. and end with an early breakfast at 2 a.m. I asked Mamaw Jo if she would cook something for the party. "Of course," Mamaw replied. "What time would I need to be there?"

"Mamaw, it doesn't start till 11 p.m.," I told her. "You don't have to come. I'll just come by and pick up the dish."

"But then I would miss out on the fun of it," Mamaw protested. "I'm not just sending the dish; I'll be there to help, honey!" My eighty-four-year-old grandmother was right there with me, serving breakfast in the middle of the night and helping me clean up at two o'clock in the morning. If you want to be an integral part of your children's and grandchildren's lives when you're eighty-four, it doesn't happen by accident; great relationships must be cultivated intentionally—as Mamaw Jo has done with each member of the family. She shows that by the time she spends with us.

Another wise eighty-four-year-old, British sculptor Henry Moore, knew the same secret Mamaw knows. The artist is quoted as having said, "The secret of life is to have a task, something you do your entire life, something you bring everything to, every minute of the day for your whole life. And the most important thing is, it must be something you cannot possibly do." I love that! Most of us are content to do what we *can*, mostly never even attempting the things we think we *cannot* do. In Mamaw's many roles of working woman, wife, mother, grandmother, and friend, I've watched her tackle many things I know she thought she could not do; it has inspired me to live my life more intentionally.

BEING INTENTIONAL IN PARENTING

Now that we've explored the concept of being intentional in other areas of life, perhaps we can more easily apply it to parenting. After we've passed through the short baby stage, when we can hardly plan beyond changing from our pajamas to the one pair of jeans that still fits, the task of getting our children to adulthood looms large. Two of my children have reached adult age and, believe me, I've asked myself tough questions like, "Did I do enough?" "Can he wash his own clothes or fry an egg?" "Can she change a tire or boil water?" When the college applications start arriving or you're addressing the wedding invitations, these questions and a thousand more will race through your mind. But by then, it's probably too late. Intentional mode must begin right after crisis mode.

If you're a new mom, congratulations! You're reading this book in time to implement many of the suggestions. If you've been a mom for a while, no problem. Start now, and your kids will reap the benefits. As we raise our kids, we must pay attention to three areas: the spiritual, the emotional, and the physical. Each area is important, and you need to set intentional goals in all areas to ensure proper growth. I can't tell you what your goals for each area should be. I can only tell you that you need to set them. You've probably heard the saying, "If you don't know where you're going, you'll probably end up somewhere else." Baseball great Yogi Berra is often credited with those true words.

Here's another quote I love. It comes from our good friend Bob

Goff: "I used to be afraid of failing at something that really mattered to me, but now I'm more afraid of succeeding at things that don't matter."[1] Think about that for a moment. We plan so many things in life; some matter and some don't. The truth is that when we don't work to do things that really matter, we end up only being successful at the things that don't. Unfortunately, all too often we don't really plan how we're going to lead our children to adulthood. But that's not going to be you. You're reading this book because you want to be intentional about instilling good character in your children. By now, you've had a chance to look over the character traits and are, hopefully, deciding which two are your top priorities. Your choices will depend on many different things, including your past experiences, your personality, and what's most important to you.

A Week of Being Intentional

One thing that has worked in our family is choosing something that I want to work on with our kids and being very intentional about it for a week. We talk about it while we're in the car and pray about it at night. When the kids were little, I would make up games that reinforced what we were trying to teach. Willie and I work together to make sure that we're modeling the characteristic and showing our children how to live it.

How can you put this into practice? For example, if sharing is a problem for your child or children, then make that your focus for a week. Be intentional about teaching the art of sharing, and make sure that you give them plenty of positive reinforcement when you see them doing it. Or you might decide that you're going to work on responsibility by making each child responsible for his or her own belongings. Talk to your children about what this means. For younger kids, set up a chart to reward and track their accomplishing tasks such as putting their shoes where they belong when they take them off. This was a big one in our home when our children were little. It drove me absolutely bonkers when we'd be ready to go and one child couldn't find his or her shoes. So as soon as they took off their shoes, we worked on training them to put them in a designated place. (Keeping me from completely losing my mind was a good enough reason to make working on this one a priority.) If the child's shoes weren't where they were supposed to be when it was time to go somewhere, the child would pay a consequence, but if the shoes were there, he or she would get a reward.

Please, don't think you should give rewards forever. I only used consequences and rewards long enough for putting their shoes away to become a habit. It would be strange to give your fifteen-year-old stickers for putting his shoes in a basket. Be aware that a skill your child conquered when he was five might become problematic again at fifteen. The child who was great at putting his things away when he was five might have a room that looks like a tornado went through it at fifteen. If so, it's time to start again. I've found that consequences seem to work better than rewards for a fifteen-year-old. In other words, your teen is more likely to respond to losing her cell phone than to a sticker chart.

Three Decisions to Set a Goal

Setting any type of goal requires making three decisions: decide what you want to achieve, decide why it matters, and decide how to make it happen. For instance, getting your child to give up the pacifier is a major step for many moms and babies. I tell parents that when they're ready to take it away, they can expect three difficult days, and then it will be over. Here's how the process I just mentioned would work: (1) decide what you want to achieve—to help your child give up the pacifier; (2) decide why it matters—it won't look good in the prom photos; and (3) decide how to make it happen—when the time comes, say to your baby in a matter-of-fact way, "Say 'bye bye' to paci" (or binky or whatever silly name you call it). Then move on. I know it won't seem like it for a few days, but the baby will be fine.

1. Decide What You Want to Achieve

     The first step sets your direction for everything that follows. Be intentional about your goal setting. Don't be wishy-washy, like the college student who constantly changes her major and ends up paying for two additional years of school. When you decide to do something worthwhile, be intentional about following through. When our youngest, Bella, was a baby, she loved pacifiers. When she got to be about eighteen months old, we decided it was time to leave the pacifiers behind. We set a goal of helping Bella get beyond her need for the comfort she obviously drew from them.

2. Decide Why It Matters

     After you've set your goal, your next step is to decide why the goal you are working for matters. Anytime we can put a "why" to a goal, it becomes more meaningful. For example, wanting to lose weight is admirable, but wanting to lose weight so you can run and play with your children gives deeper meaning to your goal. Back to the pacifier example, I knew it was time to take Bella's pacifiers away when she started carrying around three at all times—one in her mouth and one in each hand. She would even try to put two in her mouth at the same time. She was truly addicted. I wondered how she would ever learn to talk with that thing in her mouth. I knew it was time for her to give it up.

3. Decide How to Make It Happen

     Once the decision was made, we said our good-byes to the pacifiers, and they were gone—we threw them away so we wouldn't be tempted to give in and get one. We had a traumatic three days, but then it was over. Bella started talking, and she hasn't stopped since. She lost a pacifier, but she found her voice. It was a great trade-off.

Getting caught up in the busyness of today's world is the easiest way to forget your goals. We all know this from our failed list of New Year's resolutions. Still, the best strategy is to discuss your goals with your spouse and write them down. Most businesses have planning meetings to set important goals. You and your spouse can do the same thing. Get away for a weekend or one night with the goal of discussing strategies for parenting your children. Trust me, new challenges will arise every year, and you'll need to figure out how to adjust to meet your kids' needs now. You may wish to plan this to coincide with the first of the year or the beginning of the school year.

BE INTENTIONAL ABOUT BEING INTENTIONAL

It's always better to have planned what you're going to do before a situation comes up. For example, if you tell your teen to be home by 11:00 p.m. and he or she doesn't get home until midnight, what will you do? If you've discussed this with your spouse and already know what you're going to do, you can handle a potentially rocky situation with relative ease. It's even better if you've discussed the consequences ahead of time with your teen. Then there's no need for discussion or argument. If you told him or her a missed curfew would result in three days with no cell phone, simply be waiting at the door with your hand out—no discussion necessary.

Implementation is the toughest part of being intentional. Whether it's a new diet or a decision to stop a bad habit, it's easy to get bogged down in follow-through. That's why it's important to be intentional about being intentional. The success of your plan is directly correlated to the strength of your commitment and the clarity of your goal. You and your spouse must decide that good character traits are worth fighting for. Commit to living them so that your children will see them in you, and commit to helping them develop these good traits in themselves.

Willie's Words on Being Intentional

Growing up, my dad was a man's man. He would work hard and bring in the food our family would eat for dinner. He was a commercial fisherman, so he would lay out nets to catch a mess of catfish (a "mess of fish" is enough to feed the family). He would clean the fish and bring them in to Mom, who would take over from there. Mom would cook the fish and a few side dishes. My job was usually to carry out the fish guts, tossing them back in the river and cleaning off the fish table. Then one of us boys would set the table and help clean up after the meal.

So what does this have to do with being intentional? Intentional just means doing things with a purpose. My mom and dad knew that the best way to teach us boys to be men was to put us to work. I'm not sure if they sat down and had a conversation about this, but they knew it was the right thing to do.

Korie and I do sit down and talk about things we want to do with our kids. Some of the ways we teach them are just like my parents did. When John Luke shot his first deer, we were intentional about teaching him about the circle of life. We thanked him and God for providing a meal for us, and we made it special. We cooked it together, Sadie set the table, Bella made a dessert, and Will helped in the cleanup. By working together as a family, everyone did their part and they learned valuable life lessons. There will be many times in your family, like in ours, where you will need to direct what's going on. That's being intentional. If you've watched our TV show much, you know that it always ends with a message. Raising our kids is the same way. It doesn't have to seem scripted like a TV show might be, but still, you will have to direct your children for an intended outcome. If we want our TV show to go a certain direction, someone has to make that decision and implement it. If we want our kids to behave a certain way, then we have to make that decision and do the things necessary to make that happen.

Being intentional doesn't mean you live by a strict checklist.

Our family certainly doesn't do that. We're all over the place all the time. But on the important things, such as building our faith, staying strong as a family, respecting our country, and keeping our home pleasant, we stay pretty close to our checklist.

TWENTY-FOUR

NOW DO IT!

W ow! You're a busy parent, but you still found time to read this book. Why? You love your children, of course, and you want them to be strong and kind. You want them to become men and women of character. You want your little girl to grow up *strong* so she can weather any storm of adversity and come through even stronger on the other side. You want your son to be as *kind* to the man who collects the trash as to the CEO who can decide his future at the company. You want your children to be self-controlled, honest, compassionate, patient, joyful, loyal, mature, and humble—not just so that your own home will be more peaceful and enjoyable but so those character traits will be indelibly imprinted on their lives as they grow to be productive, happy adults.

You can raise this kind of children—children of character. God has given you the tools to be exactly the parent your children need. Still, good parenting is not for cowards or for the lazy. As you've been reminded in this book, raising children of good character requires thoughtful, consistent, intentional parenting. If you don't set intentional goals, how will you know how to steer your children?

WHICH TWO CHARACTER TRAITS DID YOU PICK?

At the beginning of this book, I challenged you to select two character traits you most valued for your kids and most hoped to see blossom in the adults your children will become. Then we explored what many of those traits look like.

Did you pick two? I know—we want our kids to have them all. I'm not saying that by focusing on strength and kindness (or self-control and compassion) you're letting your kids off the hook for patience, loyalty, humility, or any of the other good character traits we've discussed. Remember, the traits overlap—a kind child will show compassion and humility; a strong child will have an easier time with self-control, loyalty, patience, and honesty. But it can be overwhelming to try to focus on too many goals at once, so for now, pick two. Have it nailed down? Good.

Develop a Plan of Action

Now it's time to develop a plan of action. I've given lots of examples from my own family as to how Willie and I have tried to cultivate these character traits in our own children. Pick some of those that you think will work best for you in your situation. Hopefully, reading about our family has inspired you with some new ideas to try in similar situations you might be facing with your kids. I'm sure you have lots of great ideas that you've seen in action or that have worked well for you in the past. The key here is to decide to be proactive rather than just reacting to daily issues with your children. Talk to your children about your expectations for honesty before they have to decide how they'll explain the cookie crumbs on their lips. Figure out how you'll handle it before they have their next big meltdown at the restaurant.

Go ahead; make a game plan. Be specific. Write down the character traits you want to cultivate in your children, then your goals; then identify problem areas and outline possible solutions. No, really, do it. I'll wait.

Create a Parenting Planning Sheet

Are you ready for this next part? This is where it gets personal. Parenting kids of character doesn't work unless you and your spouse are parents of character. While you're working on how to instill values in your children, evaluate your own strengths and weaknesses as parents. In part three, we discussed the importance of being confident, consistent, loving, truthful, real, unified, creative, and intentional. We've also considered some ways to cultivate these strengths and put them into practice as parents. You might want to write each of these down in a notebook on a page labeled "My Parenting Planning Sheet" and jot down a few ways you can exercise your parenting muscles in each of these areas. Keep that plan on your nightstand or in your bathroom (wherever you like to read and where your children won't see it), and review it every once in a while. Use it to remind yourself of what you're working toward. Evaluate your progress, make any adjustments necessary, and recommit yourself daily to being a better parent in concrete, practical ways.

Good Parenting Isn't Easy, but It's Worth It

This book hasn't introduced any groundbreaking new theories or formulas for raising perfect children in five easy steps. Raising the sort of children who will have good lives, who will be the strong leaders we so desperately need today, who will enrich and strengthen the moral fiber of our nation, and who will reflect the strength and kindness of God is not easy—but it's worth it.

Statesman Frederick Douglass reportedly said, "It is easier to build strong children than to repair broken men." There's a lot of truth in that. The earlier you start, the better. But it's better to start late than never. However exceptional or broken your home or your parenting has been until now, there's no time like the present to make or renew your commitment to the process of building strong children. I hope and pray that this book has inspired and challenged you to do just that.

———

Kind heavenly Father,

Thank You for the example of love and discipline that You have set for us as parents.

Thank You for the precious gift of our dear children. You have entrusted them to our care for a season to nurture, love, and train to be good and godly men and women. Help us to remember that this is the most important and rewarding job You could have entrusted to us. May we take the responsibility seriously, committing ourselves to actively, intentionally, consistently, and lovingly parent our children. Give us wisdom and patience, grace and understanding, and joy and faith as we invite You to walk with us on this journey and dwell in our homes. Fill our homes with love, laughter, and joy. Fill our hearts with love for our children that manifests itself in doing what is best for them, even when it's hard. May we be accountable to You for our actions and the raising of our children, but may we also know Your mercy and feel Your pleasure as we strive to do our best.

Father, give the weary parent strength; infuse the discouraged parent with hope; grant the anxious parent peace. Grant us each morning the resources we need for that day and a heart of gratitude as we tuck our little ones in bed each night. Walk beside us as we walk with our children, with our eyes on the future and our knees bowed humbly before You.

In Jesus' name we pray. Amen.

APPENDIX
HOWARD FAMILY LEGACY
OF PRINCIPLES FOR LIVING

1. Actions have consequences; you reap what you sow. What you do *does* affect others. "I am responsible."
2. Respect God.
3. Family is important; there should be mutual respect and consideration within the family.
4. Respect government. Salute the position if not the person.
5. Respect your employer. Salute the position if not the person.
6. Do your duty. Some things we must do, like it or not.
7. Have faith. Trust God no matter what happens.
8. Be reverent. Worship God with all your soul, strength, and mind.
9. You have significance. You are made in the image of God.
10. We all have opportunity and the potential to do great things (risk/reward concept).
11. Be content. Happiness should not depend on your circumstances. Let it come from within.
12. Be self-disciplined. You shouldn't have to be told to control yourself.
13. Have courage. God will always be there. Take godly risks. You must step out and try things that are good.
14. Be responsible—and respond properly to your responsibilities.
15. You are not an owner but a manager. Treat all possessions as such. Give the owner (God) a fair return on His investment.

16. It's better to have little and be in Jesus than to have much and lose eternal life.
17. Be flexible.
18. Keep your priorities straight. Make first things first.
19. Recognize individual differences and accept them. Be tolerant and patient.
20. Practice active listening.
21. Be a good sharer; confess your sins, your fears, and your victories.
22. Have a sense of humor and use it correctly. Don't make fun of others.
23. Be a balanced individual. Have a balanced life.
24. Be committed to God, family, and others.
25. Always have a positive attitude and a can-do spirit.
26. Have a good prayer life. It will help you through every problem.
27. Have a healthy lifestyle. Take care of your body. Eat right and get plenty of good exercise.
28. Have an urgency for the lost.
29. Never stop learning. Get a good education and study on your own for the rest of your life.
30. Practice what you preach.
31. Don't be selfish or self-indulgent.
32. Be considerate of others and their belongings. Respect their privacy.
33. Persevere. Never give up. Be diligent.
34. Never hurt people's feelings.
35. Remember that people are more important than things.
36. Be honest and truthful. Doing what is right is never wrong!
37. Be hospitable. Open your home to others.
38. Be benevolent. Help those less fortunate. Be willing to share anything you have. Be compassionate.
39. Focus on the eternal, not the temporary.
40. Don't be afraid to be different.
41. All you need is love; love your neighbor as yourself.
42. Be gentle.

43. Never forget what Jesus did, is doing, and will do for you.

44. Be merciful and forgiving.

45. Be humble.

46. Have the heart of a servant; think like one; act like one. Don't just serve when asked.

47. Be mindful of God's creation and respect it.

48. Guard your mind. Think pure thoughts.

49. Check all beliefs and principles with the Bible.

50. If you can't say something nice, don't say anything at all. Don't gossip. If you wouldn't say it to someone's face, don't say it at all.

51. Accept criticism and correction graciously, and use it to your advantage.

52. Handle guilt; don't let it handle you.

53. Don't be afraid to admit you are wrong.

54. Say you are sorry first.

55. Don't worry. Don't be anxious.

56. Don't keep records of wrong.

57. Let Jesus be your example. Be known as a follower of Christ. Be like Him. Always ask, "What would Jesus do?"

ACKNOWLEDGMENTS

I want to start by thanking God for giving me His Son as an ultimate sacrifice, His Spirit and Word to guide me through this life, and what I'm most excited about, the hope for eternity with Him.

Next, I can't wait to thank my mom. This book would not have happened without you, not just because you helped me write it but because you taught me everything I know. I pray that I am teaching my children as joyfully, as lovingly, and as enthusiastically as you taught me. You have loved God and our family so well. Thank you for that example and for being not only my mom but also my friend.

Thank you, Dad, for your unmatched love and loyalty to God, to our family, and to your neighbor; for helping me daily in the big things and the small things. You taught me to "share and care," not to take myself too seriously, and to take God and His Word very seriously. And for that I'm eternally thankful.

A big thank-you to Phil and Miss Kay. You welcomed me into the family even though my cooking skills are still not quite up to the Robertson standard. You have taught me tons about God, love, hospitality, grace, forgiveness, joy, family, and, of course, ducks.

Thank you to Ryan and Ashley. I'm proud to call you my little bro and sis. And to our big, beautiful family—all of the Howards, Shackelfords, Owens, Kirbys, and Robertsons. I wish I could list you all by name, but that would be another book. So many amazing examples of how to live and how to love God and others. You encourage me, support me, challenge me, and cheer me on and have been doing that since the day I came into this world. I'm thankful for every family meal, birthday celebration, Scrabble tournament, basketball game, tennis match, Christmas talent show, and on and on, that I've spent with you. Life wouldn't be nearly as sweet without every single one of you.

Thank you to Debbie Wickwire and the entire W Publishing Group team. You are a joy to work with. Your love for Christ and desire to point others to Him shines through all that you do. What an honor to have gotten to know you!

Thanks to Mel Berger and Margaret Riley, always a pleasure working with you on all of the Robertson family books. It's been quite a run. Thanks for all your kindness, dedication, and hard work.

Thank you to our children—John Luke, Sadie, Will, Bella, and Rebecca. I certainly wouldn't be writing this book if it weren't for you. There is no greater joy than being your mom and seeing you grow into the men and women God desires for you to be. I learn from each of you daily. You each exemplify strong and kind in your own unique ways. You are people of good character, and I'm beyond proud to be your mom.

And last, but certainly not least, these words will never be enough, but thank you to the love of my life, Willie. You captured my heart in third grade with your charm and cute dimples. All these years later, my heart is still all yours and forever will be. So blessed to get to raise these kiddos, grow in our faith, dream big dreams, and do this life with you. Love makes things happen.

NOTES

Chapter 1: The Character Challenge

1. L. Brent Bozell III, "The Numbers on Moral Decline," Media Research Center, March 9, 2007, www.mrc.org/bozells-column/numbers-moral -decline.
2. Ibid.
3. Samir Parikh, "Preventing Youth Suicide," January 29, 2015, www.fortis healthcare.com/blog/preventing-youth-suicide.
4. George Barna, *Revolutionary Parenting* (Carol Stream, IL: Tyndale Momentum, 2010), 94.
5. Thomas Lickona, *Character Matters: How to Help Our Children Develop Good Judgment, Integrity, and Other Essential Virtues* (New York: Touchstone, 2004), 7.
6. Culture and Media Institute Staff, "The Media Assault on American Values," Media Research Center, MRC Culture, November 14, 2007, www.mrc.org/special-reports/media-assault-american-values.
7. L. Brent Bozell III, "The Numbers on Moral Decline."

Chapter 3: Make Sure You Run the Show

1. Eddie Brummelman et al., "Origins of Narcissism in Children," *Proceedings of the National Academy of Sciences of the United States of America*, vol. 112, no. 2 (March 9, 2015), 3659–62, http://www.pnas.org/content/112/12/3659.

Chapter 4: Let Your Children Grow Up

1. Dr. Michael Platt, "Myth of a Teenager," *Practical Homeschooling*, no. 2 (1993), www.home-school.com/Articles/myth-of-the-teenager.php.
2. Brooke Donatone, "Why Millennials Can't Grow Up," *Slate*, December 2, 2013, http://www.slate.com/articles/health_and_science/medical_examiner /2013/12/millennial_narcissism_helicopter_parents_are_college_students _bigger_problem.html.

3. Cindy Webb, "Overparenting Anonymous: A Parent's Guide to Letting Go," *Tulsa Kids*, March 2012, www.tulsakids.com/March-2012/Overparenting -Anonymous-A-Parents-Guide-to-Letting-Go.

Chapter 5: To Behave or Not to Behave

1. YourDictionary.com, s.v. "behave," http://www.yourdictionary.com/behave.

Chapter 7: Strong

1. *American Heritage Dictionary of the English Language*, 5th ed. (New York: Houghton Mifflin Harcourt Publishing Company, 2013), s.v. "resilience."

Chapter 8: Kind

1. *Oxford Dictionaries* (Oxford, UK: Oxford University Press, 2015), s.v. "kindness," http://www.oxforddictionaries.com/us/definition/american _english/kindness.

Chapter 9: Self-Controlled

1. *Oxford Dictionaries* (Oxford, UK: Oxford University Press, 2015), s.v. "self-control," http://www.oxforddictionaries.com/us/definition/american _english/self-control.
2. "Delaying Gratification," American Psychological Association, www.apa .org/helpcenter/willpower-gratification.pdf.

Chapter 10: Honest

1. Dictionary.com Unabridged, based on the *Random House Dictionary* (New York: Random House, 2015), s.v. "honest," http://dictionary.reference.com /browse/honest?s=t.
2. *Merriam-Webster's Collegiate Dictionary*, 11th ed. (Springfield, MA: Merriam-Webster, 2003), s.v. "dishonest," http://www.merriam-webster .com/dictionary/dishonest.
3. *Roget's 21st Century Thesaurus*, 3rd ed. (Princeton, NJ: Philip Leif Group, 2009), s.v. "dishonest," http://www.thesaurus.com/browse/dishonest?s=t.

Chapter 11: Compassionate

1. Vocabulary.com, s.v. "compassion," http://www.vocabulary.com/dictionary /compassion.

Chapter 12: Patient

1. *Merriam-Webster's Collegiate Dictionary*, 11th ed. (Springfield, MA: Merriam-Webster, 2003), s.v. "patient," http://www.merriam-webster .com/dictionary/patient.

Chapter 13: Joyful

1. *Merriam-Webster's Collegiate Dictionary*, 11th ed. (Springfield, MA: Merriam-Webster, 2003), s.v. "happy," http://www.merriam-webster.com /dictionary/happy.
2. Ibid., s.v. "joy," http://www.merriam-webster.com/dictionary/joy.
3. Christianity Stack Exchange, "What is joy? How is it different from happiness (or is it)?" October 4, 2011, http://christianity.stackexchange.com /questions/3789/what-is-joy-how-is-it-different-from-happiness-or-is-it.
4. Laura Hillenbrand, *Unbroken: A World War II Story of Survival, Resilience, and Redemption* (New York: Random House, 2010), 384.

Chapter 14: Loyal

1. *Oxford Dictionaries* (Oxford, UK: Oxford University Press, 2015), s.v. "loyal," http://www.oxforddictionaries.com/us/definition/american_english/loyal.
2. Mark Twain, *Pudd'nhead Wilson* (New York: Charles L. Webster & Company, 1894), chapter 16.

Chapter 15: Humble

1. *Oxford Dictionaries* (Oxford, UK: Oxford University Press, 2015), s.v. "esteem," http://www.oxforddictionaries.com/us/definition/american _english/esteem.
2. Ibid., s.v. "respect," http://www.oxforddictionaries.com/us/definition /american_english/respect.

Chapter 16: Be Confident

1. See also John Rosemond, *Parent-Babble* (Riverside, NJ: Andrews McMeel Publishing, 2012), front flap.

Chapter 19: Be Truthful

1. Simon Oxenham, "How Being Called Smart Can Actually Make You Stupid," http://bigthink.com/neurobonkers/how-being-called-smart-can-actually -make-you-stupid.

2. Jason Nazar, "20 Things 20-Year-Olds Don't Get," *Forbes*, July 23, 2013, http://www.forbes.com/sites/jasonnazar/2013/07/23/20-things-20-year -olds-dont-get/.

3. Geoff Colvin, *Talent Is Overrated: What Really Separates World-Class Performers from Everybody Else* (London: Portfolio, 2010).

Chapter 20: Be Real

1. Sadie Robertson, *Live Original* (Nashville: Howard Books, 2014).

2. Native American Legends, "Two Wolves," First People—The Legends, www.firstpeople.us/FP-Html-Legends/TwoWolves-Cherokee.html.

Chapter 21: Be Unified

1. *Merriam-Webster's Collegiate Dictionary*, 11th ed. (Springfield, MA: Merriam-Webster, 2003), s.v. "respect," http://www.merriam-webster .com/dictionary/respect.

Chapter 22: Be Creative

1. Betty Hart and Todd R. Risley, *Meaningful Differences in the Everyday Experience of Young American Children* (Baltimore: Paul H. Brookes, 1995), 9.

2. Ibid., 201.

Chapter 23: Be Intentional

1. Bob Goff, *Love Does* (Nashville: Thomas Nelson, 2012), 25.

ABOUT THE AUTHORS

Korie Robertson is a *New York Times* bestselling author, the wife of Duck Commander® CEO Willie Robertson, and star of A&E's *Duck Dynasty*. She balances family life and her role at Duck Commander with several other ventures, including retail store Duck and Dressing, philanthropic work in the Dominican Republic, adoption and foster care advocacy, and overseeing licensing for the family brands. Korie met Willie in third grade when he asked her to go on a moonlight hike at summer camp. They have been married since 1992 and have five children.

Chrys Howard, the mother of Korie Robertson, is the author of several books, including coauthoring the *New York Times* bestselling *Miss Kay's Duck Commander Cookbook* and *The Duck Commander Devotions for Kids*. With a degree in elementary education, she is also a teacher, public speaker, and summer camp director and has formerly served as senior editor and creative director for their family-owned business, Howard Publishing. Chrys and her husband, John, have three grown children and thirteen adorable grandchildren. They live next door to Korie and Willie in West Monroe, Louisiana.

Willie Robertson, CEO of Duck Commander®, has taken the company from a living room operation to a premiere destination for all things outdoors. *New York Times* bestselling author, executive producer of A&E's top-rated show *Duck Dynasty* and Outdoor Channel's *Buck Commander*, when not in the office or in the woods, Willie spends his time speaking all over the country, sharing the family message of faith, family, and ducks. He makes his home in West Monroe, Louisiana, with his wife, Korie, and their children: John Luke, Sadie, Will, Bella, and Rebecca.

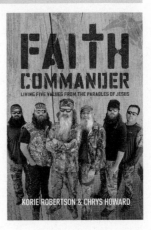